Indices:

Foreword - 6
Preface - 7
Acknowledgments - 9
Introduction - 11
The Sales Lion's Journey - 13
The Changing Landscape of Healthcare Sales - 15
Why This Book? - 17
How to Use This Book - 19
A Note on Real-Life Examples - 22

Step 1: The Foundations of Healthcare Sales - 24
- The Evolution of Healthcare Sales: A Historical Perspective - 26
- Understanding the Healthcare Landscape: Key Players and Stakeholders - 30
- The Sales Lion's Entry: Dr. Vijay Viraj's First Foray into Sales - 33
- Sales Methodologies: From Traditional to Modern Approaches - 37
- The Importance of Product Knowledge: Mastering What You Sell - 39

Step 2: Building Relationships in Healthcare - 44
- The Art of Connection: Building Trust with Healthcare Professionals - 46
- Navigating the Doctor-Salesperson Dynamic: A Unique Relationship - 49
- Networking Strategies: Expanding Your Influence - 51
- Maintaining Long-Term Relationships: Beyond the Initial Sale - 54
- Case Study: Dr. Vijay Viraj's Most Memorable Sales Interaction - 57

Step 3: Strategies for Success - 62

- Targeting the Right Audience: Identifying Potential Buyers - 64
- The Sales Lion's Playbook: Proven Techniques for Success -67
- Overcoming Objections: Handling Resistance with Grace- 70
- The Power of Presentation: Selling with Confidence - 73
- Leveraging Technology: Digital Tools for Modern Sales - 76

Step 4: Team Building and Leadership - 81
- Assembling a Winning Team: Hiring and Training the Best - 82
- The Sales Lion's Leadership Philosophy: Guiding with Vision and Purpose - 85
- Motivating Your Team: Inspiring Peak Performance - 88
- Handling Team Conflicts: Navigating Challenges for Cohesion - 91
- Celebrating Success: Recognizing and Rewarding Achievements - 93

Step 5: Analyzing the Competition - 97
- Understanding the Competitive Landscape: Who's Who in Healthcare Sales - 98
- The Sales Lion's Competitive Edge: Standing Out in a Crowded Field - 101
- Learning from Competitors: Adapting and Innovating - 104
- Strategic Positioning: Carving Out Your Niche - 107
- Case Study: Outperforming a Major Competitor - 110

Step 6: Operational Excellence - 116
- Streamlining Sales Processes: Efficiency and Effectiveness - 117
- The Role of Data: Informed Decision-Making - 120

- Supply Chain Management: Ensuring Product Availability - 123
- Feedback Loops: Continuous Improvement in Operations - 126
- The Sales Lion's Operational Mastery: Best Practices for Success - 129

Step 7: Expanding Horizons: Global Sales and Diversification - 136
- Entering New Markets: Strategies for Global Expansion - 137
- Cultural Sensitivity in Sales: Adapting to Diverse Audiences - 140
- The Sales Lion's Global Adventures: Lessons from International Sales - 143
- Diversifying Product Offerings: Expanding Your Portfolio - 146

Step 8: The Art of Negotiation - 151
- Setting the Stage: Preparing for High-Stakes Discussions - 152
- The Sales Lion's Negotiation Tactics: Winning Deals without Losing Ground - 155
- Understanding the Other Side: Empathy in Negotiation - 158
- Sealing the Deal: Closing Techniques for Success - 161
- Post-Negotiation Reflections: Learning and Growing from Every Interaction - 164
- Types of Negotiations Skills and Strategies - 167

Step 9: Adapting to Market Changes - 173
- The Ever-Changing Healthcare Landscape: Staying Updated - 174
- Innovation in Sales: Embracing New Techniques and Technologies - 177
- The Sales Lion's Adaptability: Thriving in a Dynamic Environment - 179

- Predicting Market Shifts: Being One Step Ahead - 182
- Reinventing the Sales Approach: Pivoting When Necessary - 184

Step 10: Building a Personal Brand - 192
- The Power of Personal Branding: Standing Out in a Crowded Field - 194
- Crafting the Sales Lion Image: Dr. Vijay Viraj's Branding Journey - 197
- Engaging with Your Audience: Building a Loyal Following - 199
- Leveraging Digital Platforms: Online Branding Strategies - 201
- Consistency in Branding: Maintaining a Cohesive Image - 203

Step 11: Ethics and Integrity in Sales - 208
- The Moral Compass: Navigating Ethical Dilemmas - 210
- The Sales Lion's Code of Conduct: Selling with Integrity - 213
- Building Trust through Transparency: Honesty in Sales - 216
- Handling Ethical Challenges: Case Studies and Reflections - 219
- The Long-Term Impact of Ethical Sales: Building a Lasting Legacy - 222

Step 12: The Unexpected Opportunity: Leveraging Sales Expertise - 227
- The Surprise Call: Seizing New Opportunities - 229
- First Impressions: Navigating Corporate Dynamics - 232
- Tailored Training: Meeting Specific Needs - 234
- Unveiling Surprises: The Unexpected Turn of Events - 239
- The Journey of Discovery: From Skepticism to Admiration - 241

Step 13: Continuous Learning and Growth - 246
- The Importance of Lifelong Learning: Staying at the Top of Your Game - 248
- The Sales Lion's Learning Routine: Dr. Vijay Viraj's Commitment to Education - 250
- Attending Workshops and Seminars: Expanding Your Knowledge Base - 252
- Learning from Failures: Embracing Mistakes as Growth Opportunities - 254
- Setting New Goals: The Path Forward for Continuous Achievement - 256

Conclusion/Epilogue - 262
Acknowledgments - 264
Further Reading - 266
Workbook/Action Steps - 268
About the Author - 272
Invitation for Feedback - 273
Notes/References - 274

Foreword

In the ever-evolving world of healthcare sales, few have managed to carve a niche for themselves as effectively and impactfully as Dr. Vijay Viraj. His moniker, the "Sales Lion," isn't just a title; it's a testament to his prowess, dedication, and unparalleled expertise in the field. When I was approached to pen the foreword for this book, I felt both honored and compelled, having witnessed firsthand the transformative power of Dr. Viraj's strategies.

"***High Altitude Sales: A Tale of Strategy, Secrets, and Success***" is not just another sales manual. It's a journey, a narrative, and a masterclass rolled into one. Through the engaging story of a serendipitous meeting on a flight to the USA, Dr. Viraj unravels the intricacies of healthcare sales, offering readers a unique blend of storytelling and actionable insights.

For those new to the healthcare sales industry, this book will serve as a compass, guiding you through the challenges and opportunities that lie ahead. For seasoned professionals, it offers a fresh perspective, challenging established norms and urging you to think outside the box.

But beyond the strategies and insights, what truly sets this book apart is its heart. Dr. Viraj's passion for the industry and genuine desire to uplift others shine through on every page. His anecdotes, stemming from years of experience, resonate with authenticity, making the lessons memorable and impactful.

As we stand on the cusp of a new era in healthcare sales, driven by technological advancements and changing consumer behaviors, the need for guidance has never been more critical. And who better to lead the way than the Sales Lion himself?

I urge you to dive into this book with an open mind and heart. Let the narrative captivate you, the strategies empower you, and Dr. Viraj's wisdom guide you. Here's to soaring to new heights in healthcare sales!

— Shammi Gambhir, Managing Director, Unicorn Denmart Ltd

Preface

The world of healthcare sales is as vast as it is intricate. It's a realm where science meets commerce, where innovation intertwines with tradition, and where every interaction can mean the difference between success and stagnation. As I sit down to pen this preface, I'm reminded of my own journey — a journey filled with challenges, learnings, and countless moments of epiphany.

When I first stepped into the healthcare sales arena, I was armed with nothing but raw passion and a determination to make a mark. Over the years, as I navigated the labyrinth of medical, surgical, dental, and pharma sales, I realized that this industry was unlike any other. The stakes were high, the dynamics ever-changing, and the need for a nuanced approach paramount.

"High Altitude Sales: A Tale of Strategy, Secrets, and Success" is my attempt to encapsulate those years of experience into a narrative that's both engaging and enlightening. But why a narrative, you might wonder? Why not a straightforward guide or manual? The answer is simple: Stories have the power to resonate, inspire, and stay with us long after the last page is turned.

Through the tale of a chance encounter on a transcontinental flight and the ensuing days in the vibrant city of New York, I've endeavored to distill the essence of healthcare sales. The conversations, the shared meals, the moments of revelation — they're all symbolic of the larger journey every healthcare sales professional undertakes.

This book is more than just my story. It's a reflection of the collective experiences of countless professionals who've trodden the path of healthcare sales. It's a tribute to the mentors who guided me, the peers who challenged me, and the novices who looked up to me.

As you delve into the chapters that follow, I hope you find answers to the questions that have long eluded you. I hope you discover strategies that propel you forward and anecdotes that resonate with your own experiences. But most importantly, I hope you find the inspiration to become the "Sales Lion" you were always meant to be.

Here's to a journey of discovery, growth, and unparalleled success.

Acknowledgments

The journey of writing "High Altitude Sales: A Tale of Strategy, Secrets, and Success" has been one of introspection, discovery, and gratitude. As I pause to reflect on the myriad influences that have shaped my thoughts, my career, and this book, there are a few names that stand out, deserving special mention.

First and foremost, I owe a debt of gratitude to my father. His unwavering belief in hard work, his relentless pursuit of excellence, and his indomitable spirit have been the bedrock of my values. His teachings, both spoken and unspoken, have been my guiding light, illuminating the path even in the darkest of times.

Mr. Shammi Gambhir, Founder and MD of Unicorn Denmart Ltd, has been a mentor in the truest sense of the word. His insights into the world of healthcare sales, his visionary leadership, and his ability to see potential where others saw challenges have been instrumental in shaping my professional trajectory. I am deeply thankful for his guidance and trust.

Mr. Rajesh Motwani, the former Sales Director of Vatech India, has been another pillar of support. His pragmatic approach to sales, combined with his vast reservoir of industry knowledge, has been a source of constant learning. His encouragement and constructive feedback have played a pivotal role in my growth as a sales professional.

Ron Malhotra's teachings have been a beacon, guiding me through the complexities of sales strategies and personal growth. His wisdom, gleaned from years of experience and observation, has enriched my understanding of the sales landscape.

Lastly, Dan Lok, whose writings and teachings have been a treasure trove of sales techniques and motivational insights. His ability to break down complex concepts into actionable steps has been invaluable, and his influence on this book is undeniable.

To all these stalwarts, and to countless others who've been a part of my journey, directly or indirectly, I extend my heartfelt gratitude. This book is as much yours as it is mine.

— Dr. Vijay Viraj

Introduction

In the vast expanse of the sales universe, there exists a niche that is as challenging as it is rewarding: healthcare sales. It's a realm where the stakes are high, the dynamics ever-evolving, and the players perpetually on their toes. "High Altitude Sales: A Tale of Strategy, Secrets, and Success" is not just a book; it's a voyage into this intricate world, seen through the lens of my experiences, learnings, and interactions.

As you turn the pages, you'll find yourself aboard a flight from India to the USA, seated next to a young, enthusiastic woman who's just set foot in the healthcare sales industry. Our conversations, spanning the duration of the flight and the subsequent days in the vibrant city of New York, form the crux of this narrative. But this isn't just a tale of two individuals; it's a deep dive into the strategies, operations, team-building exercises, competitor analyses, and the myriad nuances that define healthcare sales.

Why is this journey significant? Because the healthcare industry is not just about selling products; it's about impacting lives. Every sale has the potential to influence patient care, introduce innovations to medical practitioners, and shape the future of medical treatments. In such a scenario, understanding the intricacies of sales becomes paramount. This book aims to bridge the gap between theoretical knowledge and practical application, between traditional sales techniques and the unique demands of the healthcare sector.

Today, as the healthcare landscape undergoes rapid transformations, being equipped with the right sales strategies can make all the difference. Whether you're a seasoned sales professional, a newcomer to the industry, or someone curious about the behind-the-scenes workings of healthcare sales, this book promises insights that are both timeless and timely.

So, fasten your seatbelts and prepare for takeoff. The world of healthcare sales awaits, with its challenges, its triumphs, and its invaluable lessons. Welcome to "High Altitude Sales."

— Dr. Vijay Viraj

The Sales Lion's Journey

Every journey begins with a single step, and mine began in the bustling streets of India, amidst the symphony of honking vehicles, lively marketplaces, and the ever-present hum of life. As a young dental graduate, I was eager, ambitious, and ready to make my mark in the world. Little did I know that my path would lead me to the challenging yet rewarding realm of healthcare sales.

My initiation into this industry was not a product of meticulous planning but rather a serendipitous twist of fate. I was introduced to the world of medical-dental devices, pharmaceuticals, and the intricate dance of selling them. The stakes were high; every deal was not just about numbers but about potentially saving lives, improving patient care, and pioneering medical advancements.

As I navigated the complexities of this sector, I quickly realized that healthcare sales were not just about selling a product; it was about selling a vision, a promise of better healthcare, and a commitment to excellence. It demanded a deep understanding of the medical landscape, the needs of healthcare professionals, and the ever-evolving demands of patients.

Over the years, I encountered numerous challenges. From understanding the psychology of doctors to devising strategies that resonated with their needs, from competing in a saturated market to building lasting relationships, every day was a learning experience. But with challenges came growth. With every setback, I emerged stronger, more resilient, and more determined.

My moniker, "The Sales Lion," was not just a title but a testament to my journey. Like the lion, I learned to lead with courage, to navigate the terrains of the healthcare jungle, and to emerge as a leader in my domain. My rapid ascent from a sales executive to National Sales Head and then to Vice President in just 5 years (including the COVID phase) was not just a testament to my sales acumen but also to my relentless pursuit of excellence.

This book is not just a reflection of my journey but also a culmination of the lessons I've learned, the strategies I've employed, and the insights I've gained. As we embark on this narrative voyage, I invite you to see the world of healthcare sales through my eyes, to experience the highs and lows, and to discover the secrets that have made me the Sales Lion.

— Dr. Vijay Viraj

The Changing Landscape of Healthcare Sales

The world of healthcare sales is as dynamic as it is intricate. Over the years, it has undergone significant transformations, each phase bringing with it new challenges and opportunities. As we delve into this ever-evolving landscape, it's essential to understand its past, present, and the potential future.

The Past:

In the early days, healthcare sales were straightforward. The focus was primarily on the product, its features, and its benefits. Sales representatives would present their offerings, often relying on brochures and face-to-face interactions. The relationship between the salesperson and the healthcare professional was paramount, built on trust and mutual respect. The industry was less saturated, and the competition, though present, was not as fierce.

The Shift:

As the years progressed, technological advancements began to reshape the industry. The advent of digital technology brought about a paradigm shift. Sales presentations transitioned from brochures to digital platforms, and data analytics started playing a pivotal role in understanding market trends and customer behaviors. The pre-digital era's product-centric approach began to wane, making way for a more customer-centric strategy. The sales process became more nuanced, with a focus on understanding the unique needs of healthcare professionals and tailoring solutions accordingly.

The Present:

Today, the healthcare sales landscape is more complex than ever. With a plethora of products and services available, healthcare professionals are inundated with choices. The challenge now is not just to sell a product but to differentiate it, to showcase its unique value proposition. Sales representatives need to be more than just product experts; they need to be consultants, understanding the challenges faced by healthcare professionals and offering solutions that address those specific needs.

Moreover, the rise of digital platforms has transformed the way sales are conducted. Virtual meetings, webinars, and online presentations have become the norm, especially in the wake of global events like the COVID-19 pandemic. The emphasis now is on creating meaningful digital engagements that resonate with the target audience.

The Future:

As we look ahead, the future of healthcare sales is poised for further transformation. Artificial intelligence, machine learning, and advanced data analytics will play a pivotal role in understanding customer behaviors and predicting market trends. Personalized sales approaches, tailored to the individual needs of healthcare professionals, will become the gold standard. Sustainability, both in terms of products and sales practices, will gain prominence.

In this ever-changing landscape, the key to success lies in adaptability. Embracing change, staying abreast of industry trends, and continuously evolving one's sales strategies will be paramount. As we navigate this journey, it's essential to remember that at the heart of every sale is a commitment to better healthcare, improved patient outcomes, and a brighter future for all.

Why This Book?

In the vast expanse of literature on sales and marketing, countless books offer strategies, techniques, and insights. So, one might wonder, what sets this book apart? Why embark on this particular journey with me, Dr. Vijay Viraj, the Sales Lion of the healthcare industry?

A Unique Blend of Storytelling and Practical Wisdom:

At its core, this book is not just a guide; it's a narrative. It's a journey aboard a flight from India to the bustling streets of New York, where two individuals from different walks of life come together. Their conversations, set against the backdrop of the city's iconic landmarks, unravel the intricate tapestry of healthcare sales. But this isn't just any conversation; it's a masterclass, a deep dive into the world of healthcare sales, presented in a format that's both engaging and enlightening.

Real-world Insights:

While the narrative is fictional, the insights are real. They are born from my years of experience in the field, from the challenges I've faced, the successes I've celebrated, and the lessons I've learned. Every strategy discussed, and every piece of advice imparted is rooted in real-world scenarios, ensuring that readers not only enjoy the story but also derive tangible value from it.

For the Novice and the Veteran:

copyright@DrVijayViraj

Whether you're just stepping into the world of healthcare sales or have been navigating its waters for years, this book offers something for everyone. For the novice, it provides a foundation, a primer on the essentials of healthcare sales. For the veteran, it offers a fresh perspective, challenging established norms and encouraging innovative thinking.

Beyond Just Sales:

While the primary focus is on healthcare sales, the principles and strategies discussed transcend the industry. They delve into the realms of psychology, relationship-building, and personal growth. This book is as much about personal development as it is about professional success.

In essence, this book is an invitation. An invitation to view the world of healthcare sales through a different lens, to challenge the status quo, and to embark on a journey of continuous learning and growth. It's an amalgamation of storytelling and practical wisdom, designed to inspire, educate, and empower.

So, why this book? Because it's not just a book; it's an experience. An experience that promises to transform the way you view sales, relationships, and success.

How to Use This Book

Welcome to a transformative journey through the world of healthcare sales. As you delve into the pages of this book, you'll find a unique blend of narrative storytelling and actionable insights. Whether you're a novice just stepping into the realm of healthcare sales or a seasoned professional with years of experience under your belt, this book is designed to cater to your specific needs. Here's a guide on how to make the most of it:

1. Approach with an Open Mind:

The narrative format of this book is unconventional, but it's purposefully so. Allow yourself to be immersed in the story, and you'll find that the lessons resonate on a deeper level.

2. For Beginners:

If you're new to healthcare sales, start with the foundational chapters that lay the groundwork for the industry.

Pay special attention to the conversations and scenarios presented in the narrative, as they offer real-world examples of challenges and solutions.

Utilize the practical tips and strategies provided at the end of each chapter to start building your sales toolkit.

3. For Seasoned Professionals:

If you're an experienced salesperson, focus on the advanced strategies and deeper insights that are woven into the narrative.

Challenge your existing beliefs and practices. This book offers a fresh perspective, and you might find new techniques that can be integrated into your current approach.

Reflect on the conversations and scenarios, drawing parallels to your own experiences, and consider how you might handle similar situations.

4. Engage Actively:

At the end of each chapter, you'll find reflection questions and exercises. Take the time to engage with these. They're designed to help you internalize the lessons and apply them to your own sales journey.

5. Revisit Often:

The world of sales is dynamic, and as you progress in your career, you'll face new challenges and scenarios. This book is not just a one-time read. Keep it handy and revisit sections as needed. The insights and strategies provided will remain relevant, offering guidance at every stage of your career.

6. Share and Discuss:

Engage with colleagues and peers. Discuss the scenarios, strategies, and insights presented in the book. Sharing perspectives can lead to deeper understanding and innovative solutions to real-world challenges.

7. Implement and Reflect:

Reading is just the first step. The true value of this book lies in its implementation. As you apply the strategies and insights in

copyright@DrVijayViraj

your professional life, take the time to reflect on the outcomes. Adjust and adapt as needed.

Remember, this book is more than just a guide; it's a companion on your journey to becoming a Sales Lion in the healthcare industry. Approach it with curiosity, engage with it actively, and let it inspire and guide you every step of the way.

— Dr. Vijay Viraj

A Note on Real-Life Examples

As you embark on this journey through the pages of this book, you'll find yourself immersed in a narrative that weaves together the tale of a flight, a chance encounter, and enlightening conversations over dinners and coffee tables. While the storyline and some characters are products of fiction, I want to emphasize a crucial aspect: the strategies, insights, and examples presented are deeply rooted in real-life experiences and scenarios.

The world of healthcare sales is vast and intricate, and over the years, I've had the privilege of navigating its complexities firsthand. The challenges faced, the strategies employed, the successes celebrated, and the lessons learned have all been drawn from the rich tapestry of my own journey and the journeys of many professionals I've had the honor of interacting with.

Every conversation in this book, every piece of advice shared, and every strategy discussed is a reflection of genuine experiences from the field. They represent the collective wisdom of countless sales professionals, industry experts, and leaders who have graced the healthcare sales domain with their expertise.

So, while you enjoy the narrative and the unfolding story, I encourage you to approach the insights and examples with the understanding that they are not merely theoretical constructs. They are practical, tested, and proven methodologies that have been employed by real individuals in real situations. They carry the weight of years of experience, trials, errors, and triumphs.

It's my hope that by blending this real-world knowledge with a fictional narrative, the lessons will resonate more deeply, making them both memorable and actionable for you.

Here's to merging the worlds of story and strategy, and to your success in the realm of healthcare sales.

— Dr. Vijay Viraj

Step 1: The Foundations of Healthcare Sales

In the vast and intricate world of sales, the healthcare sector stands out as one of the most challenging yet rewarding domains. The stakes are high, the products and services are complex, and the customers—be they doctors, hospitals, or patients—are discerning and driven by a unique set of needs and concerns. To excel in healthcare sales, one must not only be a skilled salesperson but also possess a deep understanding of the healthcare landscape.

Step 1 of our journey delves into the very foundations of healthcare sales. It's not just about selling a product; it's about understanding the history, the key players, the ever-evolving dynamics, and most importantly, the profound impact of what's being sold. Every drug, every device, every service has the potential to change lives, and that's a responsibility no salesperson should take lightly.

In this step, we'll trace the evolution of healthcare sales, offering a historical perspective that sheds light on how past developments shape current practices. We'll introduce you to the key players and stakeholders, helping you understand their roles, motivations, and the challenges they face. Through the lens of Dr. Vijay Viraj's personal journey, you'll get a firsthand look at the trials, tribulations, and triumphs of a sales lion making his first foray into this dynamic field.

Furthermore, we'll delve into sales methodologies, transitioning from traditional approaches to modern techniques that resonate with today's healthcare professionals. And because knowledge is power, we'll emphasize the critical importance of mastering the products and services you're selling.

As we embark on this foundational step, remember that healthcare sales is not just a profession; it's a calling. It demands passion, dedication, and a relentless commitment to learning and growth. So, let's dive in and lay the groundwork for a successful journey in the world of healthcare sales.

Chapter 1: The Evolution of Healthcare Sales: A Historical Perspective

As the plane soared above the clouds, the vast expanse of the sky outside the window seemed to mirror the limitless possibilities that lay ahead. Dr. Vijay Viraj, comfortably seated in business class, took a moment to reflect on his journey in healthcare sales. The hum of the plane's engines provided a soothing backdrop to his thoughts.

Across the aisle, a young woman, perhaps in her mid-thirties, was engrossed in a book. The title caught Vijay's eye: "The Art of Selling in the Modern Age" by Robert J. Moore. It was a book he was familiar with, having read it during the early days of his career. Sensing an opportunity to strike up a conversation, Vijay leaned over and said, "That's a great read. Are you in sales?"

She looked up, a bit surprised, and replied, "Yes, I've just started in the healthcare sales industry. I'm trying to understand the landscape better."

Vijay smiled, "My name is Dr Vijay Viraj. Well, you're in for an interesting journey. If you allow, let me take you back a bit and give you a historical perspective."

She nodded.

A Glimpse into the Past

The healthcare sales industry, like many others, has its roots deeply embedded in traditional sales methods. In the early days, sales representatives would travel from town to town, carrying samples of medical and surgical equipment, and showcasing them to doctors, hospitals, and clinics. The primary focus was on the product, with little emphasis on understanding the needs of the customer.

Reference: 'The Art of Selling: A Historical Overview' by John A. Stevenson

The Rise of Specialized Healthcare Industries

As the years progressed, the healthcare sector began to diversify. The emergence of specialized fields like dental, pharma, and surgical equipment sales led to a more segmented market. Sales representatives now had to tailor their approach to cater to the specific needs of each segment.

For instance, in the dental industry, the introduction of innovative products like digital X-ray machines and laser treatments required sales reps to have a deep understanding of the technology. Similarly, in the pharma sector, the rise of personalized medicine meant that sales strategies had to be more patient-centric.

Fact: By 1985, the global pharmaceutical market was worth approximately $100 billion, with the U.S. accounting for nearly 40% of the total sales.

The Shift in Sales Dynamics

The advent of the digital age brought about a significant shift in the sales dynamics. Traditional face-to-face interactions were now complemented by digital platforms. Healthcare professionals could now access product information, reviews, and even training online. This shift meant that sales representatives had to be more knowledgeable, not just about the product, but also about the industry trends and the challenges faced by healthcare professionals.

Reference: 'Digital Transformation in Sales' by Maria Thompson

The Role of Regulatory Bodies

Another crucial aspect of the evolution of healthcare sales has been the role of regulatory bodies. With stricter regulations in place, sales representatives had to ensure that they were not just selling a product but were also providing a solution that was compliant with the latest guidelines.

For example, in the medical equipment industry, the introduction of regulations around device safety and efficacy meant that sales strategies had to focus on showcasing the product's compliance with these standards.

The Modern-Day Sales Lion

As concluded my overview, I emphasized, "Today, the role of a sales representative in the healthcare industry is not just about selling a product. It's about understanding the needs of the customer, being aware of the industry trends, and providing a solution that adds value. And that's what being a Sales Lion is all about."

The young woman, clearly intrigued, nodded in agreement. As the plane continued its journey towards New York, she realized that this trip was going to be a transformative experience, not just for her career but for her understanding of the healthcare sales industry. She remarked, "It's fascinating to see how the industry has evolved. And it's clear that to succeed, one needs to understand the past, be aware of the present, and anticipate the future."

I nodded in agreement, "Absolutely. As we delve deeper into the world of healthcare sales, you'll see how each era has its lessons, strategies, and insights. But remember, at the core of it all is the art of building genuine relationships."

Key Learning:

In "The Art of Selling in the Modern Age," Robert J. Moore emphasizes the importance of understanding the evolution of sales. He states "To be effective in sales today, one must be a student of the past, an observer of the present, and a visionary of the future."

The healthcare sales industry has evolved from a product-centric approach to a more holistic, solution-oriented strategy. To be successful in this industry, one needs to be adaptable, knowledgeable, and always willing to learn.

Reference: 'The Modern Sales Representative: Strategies and Insights' by Alan P. Roberts

Fact: According to a study by the Harvard Business Review, sales representatives who possess a deep understanding of their product and its historical context are 32% more likely to close deals compared to those who don't.

Stay tuned for the next chapter, where we delve into the intricate landscape of healthcare and the key players that shape it.

Chapter 2: Understanding the Healthcare Landscape: Key Players and Stakeholders

The hum of the airplane's engines provided a soothing backdrop as the young woman, intrigued by my insights, leaned in closer. "Dr. Viraj," she began, "I've always been curious about the broader healthcare landscape. Who are the major players, and how do they interact?"

Dr. Viraj smiled, appreciating her thirst for knowledge. "Let's break it down," I began.

1. Healthcare Providers

"First and foremost, we have the healthcare providers. These are your doctors, nurses, and other medical professionals. They're the ones directly interacting with patients and using the products we sell."

"Did you know that in the dental industry alone, there are over 300,000 practicing dentists in India and the same in the USA too?" he added, citing a statistic to emphasize the scale.

Reference: 'Dental Demographics' by Dr. Jane Smith

2. Medical Institutions

"Next, we have institutions like hospitals, clinics, and diagnostic centers. They're the infrastructure of our healthcare system. For instance, in the pharma industry, hospitals are the largest buyers, accounting for nearly 60% of total sales."

Reference: 'Pharmaceutical Sales Strategies' by Alan P. Roberts

3. Regulatory Bodies

"These are the watchdogs. They ensure that the products and services in the market are safe and compliant. In the medical equipment sector, for example, FDA approvals can make or break a product's success."

Reference: 'Navigating Medical Regulations' by Peter L. Jackson

4. Manufacturers and Distributors

"Manufacturers produce the equipment and medicines, while distributors ensure they reach the right places. A key strategy here is building strong relationships to ensure a steady supply chain."

"In the surgical equipment industry, for instance, distributors play a pivotal role, influencing over 80% of sales decisions," I added.

Reference from search results: 'Pioneering Healthcare Sales Excellence'

5. Patients and End-Users

"Lastly, we must never forget the end-users. They're the reason we're all here. Understanding their needs is paramount. For instance, in the pharma sector, patient feedback has led to the development of more user-friendly drug delivery systems."

Reference: 'Patient-Centric Pharma' by Dr. Emily R. Lewis

The young woman, absorbing the information, asked, "So, how do all these players come together?"

I responded, "It's a dance of sorts. Everyone has a role, and understanding these roles is key to mastering sales in the healthcare sector."

She nodded, jotting down notes, eager to delve deeper into the world of healthcare sales.

Chapter 3: The Evolution of a Sales Lion: Dr. Vijay Viraj's Journey Through the Healthcare Sales

The airplane's gentle turbulence momentarily interrupted their conversation. As the plane stabilized, the young woman's curiosity was evident. "Dr. Viraj," she began, "how did you evolve in the vast healthcare sales landscape? What were the key milestones in your journey?"

Dr. Viraj chuckled, reminiscing about his early days. "Ah, the evolution of the Sales Lion," he mused.

1. The Foundation: Medical Beginnings

"My journey began as a Junior Resident at VMMC & Safdarjang Hospital, where I attended to patients and devised treatment plans. This experience laid the foundation for my understanding of the medical field. It was during this time I realized the importance of patient-centric care and the role of effective communication in healthcare."

2. The Shift to Administration

"After my residency, I ventured into hospital administration at Apollo Hospitals. Here, I managed medical tourism and hospital administration, which gave me insights into the business side of healthcare. This role taught me the intricacies of healthcare management and the importance of streamlining processes for better patient outcomes."

3. The Dive into Insurance

"Post Apollo, I transitioned to Raksha TPA Private Ltd. as a Medical Advisor, handling medical claims and training new employees. My subsequent roles at Medi Assist and Health Insurance TPA of India Ltd. further deepened my understanding of the insurance landscape. I learned the significance of timely claim settlements and the role of TPAs in bridging the gap between insurance companies and policyholders."

4. The Dental Radiology Expertise

"At Unicorn Denmart Ltd., I specialized in dental radiology products. I conducted product demonstrations, trained sales teams, and developed sales channel frameworks. My expertise in 3D rendering and CBCT software applications became pivotal. The dental industry was evolving rapidly, and I was determined to ensure that our products were at the cutting edge."

5. The E-Commerce Revolution

"My foray into e-commerce began as a Digital Sales Manager, where I focused on business expansion strategies. Later, as a Business Consultant for Collateral Medical Private Limited, I strategized and executed e-commerce business plans. The digital age was reshaping the healthcare industry, and I was at the forefront, harnessing the power of technology to enhance patient care."

6. The Entrepreneurial Leap

"My entrepreneurial journey began with the Sales Lion Club and Bada Employee. As a Business Mentor, I empowered individuals in the healthcare industry, providing tailored guidance and mentorship. My mission with Badaemployee.com was to help employees achieve financial and career growth. Entrepreneurship taught me resilience, adaptability, and the importance of continuous learning."

7. The Learning and Development Era

"In July 2022, I took on the role of Learning and Development Consultant at Eleserv Softech Pvt Ltd. Here, I was deeply involved in designing, implementing, and managing learning and development programs. My aim was to enhance employee skills, knowledge, and performance within the company. This role was a testament to my commitment to fostering a culture of continuous learning and professional growth.

8. The Clear Aligners Leadership

Subsequently, I held prestigious positions as the National Sales Head at ODS Clear Aligners (In 2022) and Vice President of Business Expansion at 32 Watts Clear Aligners (In 2023). These roles required a deep understanding of the dental industry, especially the rapidly growing clear aligners segment. My responsibilities included driving sales strategies, expanding business operations, and ensuring that our products met the highest standards of quality and efficacy. The clear aligners market is a dynamic one, and my expertise in sales and marketing played a pivotal role in navigating its challenges.

9. The Current Role: Head of Marketing

"Currently, as the Head of Marketing at Unicorn Denmart Ltd., I drive impactful strategies for business growth, transforming visions into successful campaigns and building solid connections in the industry. Marketing is not just about selling products; it's about telling a story, building relationships, and creating value for customers."

The young woman, clearly inspired, remarked, "Your journey is a testament to the fact that with the right approach and mindset, one can achieve greatness in any field."

Dr. Viraj nodded, "Indeed. And remember, every professional's journey is unique. It's about finding your path and walking it with determination."

Chapter 4: Sales Methodologies: From Traditional to Modern Approaches

The hum of the airplane's engines was a constant backdrop as Dr. Viraj and the young woman beside him continued their conversation. She leaned in, curiosity evident in her eyes. "Dr. Viraj, I've always been intrigued by the evolution of sales methodologies. How have they changed over time, especially in specialized sectors like dental, medical, and pharma?"

Dr. Viraj, appreciating the depth of her question, replied, "Sales methodologies have indeed evolved, reflecting the changing dynamics of the market and customer behavior. Let's journey through the transformation."

1. Traditional Sales Methodologies

"Initially, sales were straightforward and product-centric. The emphasis was on what the product could do."

A. Feature-Benefit Selling: "This method is foundational. For instance, in the dental industry, a toothbrush might have 'soft bristles' (feature) that ensure 'gentle cleaning' (benefit)."

B. Solution Selling: "This approach, emerging in the 1980s, shifted the focus from products to solutions. Instead of merely selling a medical device, reps would identify a doctor's challenge and offer a solution."

Key Learning from "Solution Selling" by Michael T. Bosworth: "Tailoring your solution to address specific customer pain points leads to more successful sales outcomes."

2. Modern Sales Methodologies

"As the market grew more competitive, sales methodologies became more customer-centric."

A. Consultative Selling: "Here, the salesperson acts more as a consultant. In the pharma sector, it's about understanding a doctor's needs and offering tailored advice."

B. Inbound Selling: "With the digital age, customers began their research online. This method attracts customers through informative content. For surgical equipment, it could be through webinars or online demos."

C. Value-Based Selling: "This focuses on the value a product brings. In the medical equipment domain, it's not just about features but how a device can enhance patient care."

Key Learning from "SPIN Selling" by Neil Rackham: "Understanding and addressing the explicit and implicit needs of customers can significantly improve sales success."

The young woman pondered, "So, it's not just about pushing a product but understanding the customer's needs?"

"Exactly," I nodded, "And as markets and technologies evolve, so will sales methodologies. The key is to remain adaptable and always prioritize the customer's needs."

She smiled, jotting down notes, "This is invaluable, Dr. Viraj. I can see how these methodologies can be applied across industries, especially in specialized sectors."

I grinned, "And that's just the beginning. Sales is an ever-evolving field, and there's always more to learn and adapt."

The conversation flowed, the miles flew by, and the journey of sales exploration continued.

Chapter 5: The Importance of Product Knowledge: Mastering What You Sell

The airplane's cabin lights dimmed, signaling that most passengers were settling into a restful slumber. But for me and the young woman, the journey of knowledge was far from over.

She leaned in, her notebook filled with scribbles from their previous discussions. "Dr. Viraj, I've always believed that to sell something effectively, you need to know it inside out. How crucial is product knowledge in sales?"

Dr. Viraj, adjusting his seat for comfort, began, "Product knowledge is the backbone of effective sales. Let's delve deeper."

1. Confidence in Conversations

"Knowing your product gives you confidence. Whether you're selling dental instruments or pharmaceutical drugs, understanding the intricacies allows you to answer questions and handle objections with ease."

Q: "But can't we just rely on product brochures or manuals?"

A: "While they're helpful, firsthand knowledge makes your pitch more authentic and trustworthy."

2. Building Trust with Customers

"When you can discuss your product's features, benefits, and potential challenges without hesitation, customers trust you more. In the medical field, for instance, doctors rely on sales reps to provide accurate information about equipment or drugs."

Q: "So, it's about being a reliable source of information?"

A: "Absolutely. Your credibility is on the line."

3. Tailoring Your Pitch

"Every customer is unique. With in-depth product knowledge, you can tailor your pitch to suit individual needs. For example, a dentist might need a specific feature in a dental chair, and knowing your product helps you highlight that."

Q: "It's like customizing the product presentation for each client?"

A: "Exactly. It's about resonating with their specific needs."

4. Staying Ahead of the Competition

"In competitive industries, like surgical equipment, what sets you apart is not just the product but how well you can present its advantages. Deep product knowledge gives you an edge."

Q: "So, it's a competitive advantage?"

A: "Indeed. It differentiates you from others who might only have surface-level knowledge."

Key Learning from "The New Strategic Selling" by Robert B. Miller and Stephen E. Heiman: "Deep product knowledge, combined with understanding customer needs, is the key to strategic selling. It's about aligning what you sell with what your customer truly needs."

The young woman looked thoughtful, "Dr. Viraj, this makes so much sense. Product knowledge isn't just about facts and figures; it's about connecting those facts to customer needs."

I nodded in agreement, "Precisely. It's the bridge between what you offer and what your customer seeks. And mastering that bridge is the essence of successful sales."

As the plane continued its journey, so did their enlightening conversation, each topic building on the last, weaving a tapestry of sales wisdom.

Reflections on the Foundations of Healthcare Sales

The hum of the airplane's engines provided a gentle backdrop as the young woman took a moment to gather her thoughts. She turned to Dr. Viraj, her eyes sparkling with newfound knowledge. "Dr. Viraj," she began, "our discussions have been incredibly enlightening. Here's what I've gathered so far."

1. "The healthcare sales industry has evolved significantly over the years. It's not just about selling products but about providing solutions tailored to specific healthcare needs."

2. "Understanding the landscape is crucial. Knowing the key players, from manufacturers to end-users, helps in strategizing sales approaches effectively."

3. "Your journey, Dr. Viraj, taught me the importance of adaptability and resilience in sales. Every challenge faced is an opportunity to learn and grow."

4. "Sales methodologies have shifted from being product-centric to being customer-centric. It's about understanding customer pain points and addressing them."

5. "Deep product knowledge is non-negotiable. It instills confidence, builds trust, and allows for tailored pitches."

6. "The healthcare industry is unique. Its sales approaches must consider the critical nature of the products and the profound impact they have on patients' lives."

7. "Building relationships is at the heart of healthcare sales. It's not just a one-time transaction but a continuous partnership."

8. "Staying updated with the latest trends and technologies in healthcare is essential. It positions you as a knowledgeable and reliable salesperson."

9. "Strategic selling, as mentioned in 'The New Strategic Selling', is about aligning product offerings with genuine customer needs."

10. "Every customer is unique. Customizing the sales pitch to resonate with individual needs can make a significant difference."

11. "In the competitive world of healthcare sales, having an edge is vital. Deep product knowledge and understanding customer needs provide that edge."

12. "Continuous learning is the key. The healthcare industry is ever-evolving, and staying updated ensures you're always ahead of the curve."

13. "Feedback is invaluable. It provides insights into areas of improvement and helps refine sales strategies."

14. "Ethics and integrity are paramount. Given the sensitive nature of healthcare products, honesty and transparency are essential."

15. "Lastly, passion drives success. Being genuinely passionate about improving patient care through your products will shine through in every sales interaction."

The young woman paused, taking a deep breath. "These learnings have reshaped my perspective on healthcare sales. I'm eager to delve deeper and understand the next steps."

Dr. Viraj smiled warmly, "Your reflections are spot on. Let's continue our journey into the world of healthcare sales.

Step 2: Building Relationships in Healthcare

The realm of healthcare is not just about products, services, or cutting-edge innovations; at its core, it's about people. It's about the doctors who dedicate their lives to patient care, the patients who seek the best treatments, and the sales professionals who bridge the gap, ensuring that the right solutions reach the right hands. In this intricate dance, relationships are the heartbeat, the rhythm that drives success.

Step 2 invites you on a journey to explore the art and science of building and nurturing relationships in the healthcare sector. While the principles of relationship-building are universal, the healthcare industry presents its unique challenges and opportunities. Here, trust is paramount. A doctor's recommendation or a hospital's procurement decision can directly impact lives, making the stakes incredibly high.

Through this step, we'll delve into the nuances of building trust with healthcare professionals. How does one navigate the delicate dynamics between a doctor and a salesperson? What strategies can be employed to expand one's influence, not just as a sales representative but as a trusted advisor? We'll explore these questions and more, offering insights and strategies to foster genuine, long-lasting relationships.

Drawing from real-life scenarios and case studies, including Dr. Vijay Viraj's memorable interactions, we'll showcase the power of connection, empathy, and authenticity. We'll also delve into the strategies for maintaining these relationships, ensuring that they evolve and thrive beyond the initial sale.

As we journey through Step 2, remember that in healthcare sales, relationships are the foundation. They are the bridges that connect needs to solutions, challenges to innovations, and most importantly, people to people. So, let's embark on this exploration, understanding the essence of relationship-building in the world of healthcare sales.

Chapter 6: The Art of Connection: Building Trust with Healthcare Professionals

The airplane's gentle hum continued as the two conversationalists prepared to delve deeper into the intricacies of healthcare sales. I, with a playful glint in my eyes, turned to the young woman and said, "You know, we've been talking for hours, and I've shared so much about my journey, but I just realized I don't even know your name!"

The young woman chuckled, "Oh! How rude of me. I'm Aanya."

Dr. Viraj smiled, "Pleasure to officially meet you, Aanya. It's lovely to connect you. The art of connection always opens new opportunities."

Aanya: "Dr. Viraj, I've always believed that sales are not just about selling a product but building a relationship. How do you build trust, especially with healthcare professionals who are often pressed for time and skeptical of salespeople?"

"Aanya, you've hit the nail on the head. Building trust is paramount. Here's how I approach it:

1. Understand Their World: Before you can sell anything, you need to understand the daily challenges, pressures, and aspirations of healthcare professionals. This empathy forms the foundation of trust.

2. Be Genuine: Healthcare professionals have a keen sense of insincerity. Always be genuine in your interactions. If you don't know something, admit it. If you believe a product isn't right for them, say it.

3. Provide Value: Every interaction should provide value. Whether it's sharing the latest research, offering insights into patient care, or introducing them to a product that can genuinely help, always aim to add value.

4. Listen Actively: Often, salespeople are so focused on their pitch that they forget to listen. Active listening shows respect and helps you tailor your approach to their specific needs.

5. Follow-up: Trust is built over time. Regular follow-ups, not just for sales but to check in on how they're doing or share something interesting, can go a long way."

Aanya: "That sounds comprehensive. But how do you handle skepticism, especially when introducing a new product?"

Dr. Viraj: "Skepticism is natural, especially in the healthcare industry where decisions impact patient lives. Here's my approach:

1. Be Prepared: Know your product inside out. Be ready with clinical data, patient testimonials, and any other evidence that supports your claims.

2. Address Concerns Head-On: If a healthcare professional has reservations, address them directly. Provide evidence, offer trials, or connect them with peers who've had positive experiences with the product.

3. Be Patient: Trust isn't built overnight. It's okay if a healthcare professional isn't ready to make a decision immediately. Give them time and space to consider."

Aanya: "This is enlightening, Dr. Viraj. Building trust seems like an art in itself."

Dr. Viraj: "It truly is, Aanya. And once you master this art, the world of healthcare sales opens up in ways you can't even imagine."

As the conversation flowed, Aanya felt a growing sense of admiration for Dr. Viraj's wisdom and experience. She eagerly awaited the next chapter of their journey together.

Chapter 7: Navigating the Doctor-Salesperson Dynamic: A Unique Relationship

The plane's gentle hum provided a soothing backdrop as Aanya and Dr. Viraj continued their enlightening conversation. Aanya, with a notebook now in hand, was keen to capture every nugget of wisdom Dr. Viraj shared.

Aanya: "Dr. Viraj, the relationship between a doctor and a salesperson has always intrigued me. It's not like any other sales dynamic. How do you navigate this unique relationship?"

Dr. Viraj: "Aanya, you're absolutely right. The doctor-salesperson dynamic is unique. It's a delicate balance of trust, respect, and mutual benefit.

Here's how I approach it:

1. Respect Their Time: Doctors have incredibly busy schedules. Always schedule appointments in advance, be punctual, and get to the point quickly.

2. Educate, Don't Just Sell: Doctors appreciate salespeople who can educate them about the latest advancements, research, and trends. Be a source of knowledge, not just a sales pitch.

3. Understand Their Challenges: Every doctor has unique challenges, whether it's patient care, administrative burdens, or staying updated with the latest research. Understand these challenges and tailor your approach accordingly.

4. Build Personal Connections: While the professional relationship is paramount, building personal connections can go a long way. Remembering birthdays, and anniversaries, or simply asking about their day can make a difference.

5. Always Be Ethical: The healthcare industry is built on trust. Always be transparent, honest, and ethical in your dealings."

Aanya: "It sounds like a lot of emotional intelligence is required to navigate this relationship."

Dr. Viraj: "Absolutely, Aanya. Emotional intelligence is key. It's about understanding, empathizing, and connecting on a deeper level."

Golden Rule from "The Psychology of Selling" by Brian Tracy: "People buy for emotional reasons and justify with logical ones. Understand the emotions driving the purchase."

Aanya: "That golden rule makes so much sense. It's not just about the product but the emotions and needs behind the purchase."

Dr. Viraj: "Exactly, Aanya. And when you understand those emotions and needs, you can tailor your approach, build deeper connections, and ultimately, drive sales."

As the plane soared above the clouds, Aanya felt a renewed sense of purpose and clarity. With Dr. Viraj's guidance, she was confident she could navigate the intricate world of healthcare sales with grace and success.

Chapter 8: Networking Strategies: Expanding Your Influence

As the plane continued its journey, Aanya was engrossed in the wealth of knowledge Dr. Viraj was sharing. She was eager to delve deeper into the intricacies of sales, especially in the healthcare sector.

Aanya: "Dr. Viraj, I've always believed that your network is your net worth. How do you go about expanding your influence, especially in the healthcare industry?"

Dr. Viraj: "Aanya, you've hit the nail on the head. Networking is crucial, especially in an industry as vast and interconnected as healthcare.

Here are some strategies I've employed over the years:

1. Attend Industry Conferences: These events are goldmines for networking. Not only do you get to learn about the latest trends and advancements, but you also get to meet industry leaders, potential clients, and even competitors.

2. Join Professional Associations: Being a part of associations like the Medical Sales Association or the Healthcare Businesswomen's Association can provide numerous networking opportunities.

3. Offer Value First: Instead of approaching someone with what you want, approach them with what you can offer. This could be in the form of knowledge, a connection, or even a business opportunity.

4. Leverage social media: Platforms like LinkedIn are invaluable for networking. Regularly share insights, engage with industry news, and connect with professionals in your field.

5. Build Genuine Relationships: Networking isn't just about collecting business cards. It's about building genuine, long-term relationships. Always follow up, stay in touch, and offer help when you can."

Aanya: "These strategies sound very effective. By the way, on a lighter note, did you use any of these networking or sales skills to impress your wife?"

Dr. Viraj: (Laughing) "Ah, that's an interesting story! While I didn't exactly use a sales pitch, I did use some principles of persuasion. We met at a mutual friend's party. I had just five minutes to make an impression. I complimented her on her grace and asked her about her passion for fashion and modeling. I genuinely listened to her, and by the end of our conversation, I had not only impressed her but also got her contact details."

Aanya: "Wow, just five minutes? That's impressive!"

Dr. Viraj: "Yes, and today she's not only my life partner but also a successful professional fashion model. She runs a modeling agency by the name of "Lavistyle Production" in Delhi-NCR and has been featured in the movie 'Tu Joothi Mai Makkar'. She's acted as the lead actress in over 15 album songs and has judged more than 35 fashion shows. She has done over 12 live events including beauty pageants, award shows, and talent shows. I'm incredibly proud of her achievements."

Aanya: "That's truly inspiring! It's amazing how life can surprise us in the most unexpected ways."

Dr. Viraj: "Indeed, Aanya. Life is full of surprises, and it's up to us to make the most of every opportunity."

As the conversation flowed, Aanya felt more and more inspired. Dr. Viraj's stories and insights were not just enlightening but also filled with warmth and wisdom. She was eager to learn more and apply these lessons in her own career.

Chapter 9: Maintaining Long-Term Relationships: Beyond the Initial Sale

The plane's hum provided a soothing backdrop as Aanya and Dr. Viraj continued their enlightening conversation. Aanya, with her notebook filled with insights, was eager to delve deeper into the nuances of sales.

Aanya: "Dr. Viraj, I've always believed that the real challenge in sales isn't just acquiring a customer but retaining them. How do you ensure that you maintain long-term relationships with your clients, especially in the healthcare sector?"

Dr. Viraj: "Aanya, you're absolutely right. Acquiring a new customer can cost five times more than retaining an existing one. In the healthcare industry, where trust and credibility are paramount, maintaining long-term relationships is crucial.

Here are some strategies I've employed over the years:

1. Regular Follow-ups: It's essential to check in with your clients regularly, not just when you're trying to make a sale. This shows them that you genuinely care about their needs and are not just interested in their money.

2. Provide Value Beyond the Product: This could be in the form of insights, industry news, or even training sessions. By offering additional value, you position yourself as a trusted advisor rather than just a salesperson.

3. Address Concerns Proactively: If a client has an issue with your product or service, address it immediately. This not only solves their problem but also shows them that you're committed to their satisfaction.

4. Personalize Your Interactions: Remembering small details about your clients, like their birthdays or anniversaries, can go a long way in building a personal connection."

Aanya: "These strategies sound very effective. But how do you ensure that you don't come across as too pushy or salesy?"

Dr. Viraj: "That's where the art of relationship-building comes into play. It's about striking the right balance between being professional and being genuine. Always prioritize the client's needs over your sales targets."

Golden Rule #1: "People don't care how much you know until they know how much you care." - How to Win Friends and Influence People by Dale Carnegie.

Golden Rule #2: "Trust is built with consistency." - The Speed of Trust by Stephen M.R. Covey.

Golden Rule #3: "Loyalty is not won by being first. It is won by being best." - Top Performance: How to Develop Excellence in Yourself and Others by Zig Ziglar.

Aanya: "These golden rules are truly insightful. Do you have any data or figures that highlight the importance of maintaining long-term relationships?"

Dr. Viraj: "Certainly! According to a study by Bain & Company, increasing customer retention rates by just 5% can increase profits by 25% to 95%. Furthermore, the likelihood of selling to an existing customer is 60-70%, while the likelihood of selling to a new prospect is just 5-20%."

Aanya: "Those figures are eye-opening! It truly underscores the importance of maintaining long-term relationships."

Dr. Viraj: "Indeed, Aanya. In the end, sales is not just about transactions; it's about building and nurturing relationships."

As the conversation flowed, Aanya realized that the principles Dr. Viraj was sharing were not just applicable to sales but to life in general. Building and maintaining relationships is the cornerstone of both personal and professional success

Chapter 10: Case Study: Dr. Vijay Viraj's Most Memorable Sales Interaction

The plane was now cruising smoothly, and the lights of distant cities twinkled below. Aanya, engrossed in the conversation, leaned in, eager to hear more personal experiences from Dr. Viraj.

Aanya: "Dr. Viraj, with all your years in sales, there must be some interactions that stand out. Could you share one of your most memorable sales experiences?"

Dr. Viraj: "Ah, Aanya, there are many, but one does come to mind immediately. It was early in my career, and I was trying to introduce a new dental imaging device to a renowned dental hospital in Delhi. The head dentist, Dr. Sharma, was known for being very particular and rarely changed his equipment suppliers."

Aanya: "Sounds challenging!"

Dr. Viraj: "It was. I had done my homework, knew the product inside out, and was confident about its advantages. But during our meeting, instead of diving straight into the product details, I started by asking Dr. Sharma about the challenges he faced with his current equipment."

Aanya: "A different approach!"

Dr. Viraj: "Exactly. Dr. Sharma opened up about the limitations of his current devices. This gave me a clear picture of his needs.

Instead of a generic pitch, I tailored my presentation to address each of his concerns. By the end, not only was he convinced about the product, but he also appreciated the effort I took to understand his needs."

Aanya: "So, understanding the client's needs was the key?"

Dr. Viraj: "Absolutely. And not just understanding, but genuinely caring about solving their problems. That sale taught me the importance of empathy in sales."

Golden Rule #1: "Seek first to understand, then to be understood." - The 7 Habits of Highly Effective People by Stephen R. Covey.

Golden Rule #2: "People don't buy for logical reasons. They buy for emotional reasons." - How to Master the Art of Selling by Tom Hopkins.

Golden Rule #3: "Sales success comes after you stretch yourself past your limits on a daily basis." - Sell or Be Sold by Grant Cardone.

Aanya: "These golden rules resonate so much with your story. Do you have any data that emphasizes the importance of understanding client needs?"

Dr. Viraj: "Certainly. According to a recent study by Salesforce, 79% of business buyers say it's absolutely critical or very important to interact with a salesperson who is a trusted advisor — not just a sales rep.

Another study by Accenture found that 91% of customers are more likely to buy from brands that recognize, remember, and provide them with relevant offers and recommendations."

Aanya: "Those numbers are compelling. It's clear that understanding and addressing client needs is paramount."

Dr. Viraj: "Indeed, Aanya. Sales is not just about pushing a product; it's about building trust, understanding needs, and providing solutions."

As the conversation deepened, Aanya realized that the principles of sales were intertwined with the principles of life. Building trust, understanding, and genuine care were the cornerstones of meaningful relationships, both in sales and in life.

Key Learnings from Step 2: Building Relationships in Healthcare

1. Trust is the Foundation: Building genuine trust is the cornerstone of any successful sales relationship, especially in healthcare where decisions impact patient care.
2. Understand Before Being Understood: Taking the time to truly understand the needs and concerns of healthcare professionals can set you apart in the sales process. (Reference: The 7 Habits of Highly Effective People by Stephen R. Covey)
3. The Unique Dynamic: The relationship between doctors and salespeople is unique. Recognizing the expertise and concerns of healthcare professionals is crucial to navigating this dynamic effectively.

4. Expand Your Influence: Effective networking is not just about expanding your contacts but about building meaningful, mutually beneficial relationships.
5. Beyond the Initial Sale: The real challenge in sales is not just making the initial sale but maintaining and nurturing that relationship for long-term business and referrals.

6. Empathy is Key: In sales, especially in healthcare, empathy can be a game-changer. Understanding and addressing the emotional needs of clients can lead to more successful outcomes.
7. Tailored Solutions: One-size-fits-all doesn't work in healthcare sales. Tailoring your pitch and solutions to address specific concerns is essential.

8. The Power of Personal Stories: Sharing personal experiences, like Dr. Viraj's memorable sales interaction, can make sales pitches more relatable and impactful.
9. Continuous Learning: The healthcare industry is ever-evolving. Staying updated with the latest trends, technologies, and treatments is crucial for effective sales.

10. Data-Driven Insights: Using data, like the statistics from Salesforce and Accenture, can provide credibility to your sales pitch and help address client concerns more effectively.
11. The Role of Emotions: Recognizing that sales decisions, especially in healthcare, are often driven by emotions can help in crafting a more effective sales strategy. (Reference: How to Master the Art of Selling by Tom Hopkins)
12. Long-Term Vision: Building relationships in healthcare sales is not about short-term gains but about long-term partnerships and mutual growth.

13. The Importance of Feedback: Regular feedback from healthcare professionals can provide insights into improving products, services, and sales strategies.
14. Ethical Considerations: In healthcare, ethical considerations are paramount. Ensuring that sales strategies prioritize patient care and ethical standards can build trust and credibility.
15. Adaptability: The healthcare industry, being dynamic, requires sales professionals to be adaptable, ready to learn, and quick to respond to the changing needs and concerns of healthcare professionals.

Step 3: Strategies for Success

In the vast ocean of healthcare sales, where every wave brings a new challenge and every tide tests your resilience, having a compass is essential. That compass? A well-defined strategy. While the foundation of sales lies in relationships and trust, the structure that holds it all together is built on strategic planning, execution, and adaptability.

Step 3 delves deep into the heart of sales strategies, illuminating the path for both novices and seasoned professionals. Here, we uncover the secrets of targeting the right audience, ensuring that every effort is directed towards those who genuinely need and value the solutions offered. But how does one do that in a field as vast and varied as healthcare? The answers lie within.

Drawing from Dr. Vijay Viraj's playbook, we'll explore proven techniques that have not only yielded results but have also transformed challenges into opportunities. From understanding the nuances of overcoming objections to mastering the art of presentation, this step is a treasure trove of insights and actionable advice.

In today's digital age, technology plays a pivotal role in sales. Hence, we'll also delve into the digital tools that are revolutionizing the way sales are conducted, offering efficiency, precision, and a touch of innovation.

Throughout this step, real-life scenarios and case studies will serve as beacons, guiding us through the complexities of healthcare sales. Whether it's about identifying potential buyers or leveraging the latest digital platforms, the lessons here are both timeless and timely.

As we navigate through Step 3, remember that strategy is not just about planning; it's about envisioning success, adapting to challenges, and consistently moving towards the goal. With the right strategies in place, success isn't just a possibility; it's a guarantee. So, gear up to dive deep into the world of strategic sales, where every move is calculated, every challenge is an opportunity, and success is a journey, not just a destination.

Chapter 11: Targeting the Right Audience: Identifying Potential Buyers

As the plane continued its journey, Aanya leaned in, her interest piqued. "Dr. Viraj, one of the challenges I've faced in my short sales stint is identifying the right audience. How do you ensure you're reaching out to potential buyers who are genuinely interested?"

Dr. Viraj smiled, "Ah, targeting! One of the most crucial steps in the sales process. Let's dive into it."

Understanding Your Product Inside Out

Before you can identify who would be interested in your product, you need to understand your product thoroughly. In the healthcare industry, whether you're selling medical-equipment, pharmaceuticals, or health services, you need to know the unique selling points (USPs) and benefits of what you're offering.

Defining Your Ideal Customer Profile (ICP)

An Ideal Customer Profile is a detailed description of a company or individual that would get the most value out of your product and provide value to your company in return. For instance, if you're selling premium dental equipment, your ICP might be dental clinics in urban areas with more than three dentists on staff.

Golden Rule #1: "Start with the end in mind." - The 7 Habits of Highly Effective People by Stephen R. Covey. Know who you want to target before you begin your sales process.

Segmentation is Key:

Segment your market based on various criteria:

- Demographics: Age, gender, occupation, etc.
- Geographics: Location can play a crucial role, especially in healthcare where certain products might be more relevant in specific areas.
- Behavioral Factors: Buying patterns, brand loyalty, etc.

According to a study by Salesforce, 79% of marketing leads never convert into sales. Proper segmentation can significantly improve this figure.

Research and Data Analysis

Use tools and platforms that provide insights into potential leads. Platforms like LinkedIn can be invaluable for B2B sales, helping you identify key decision-makers in organizations.

Golden Rule #2: "In God we trust; all others bring data." - Edward Deming. Rely on data-driven insights to refine your targeting strategy.

Engage and Validate

Once you've identified potential leads, engage with them. This could be through content marketing, webinars, or direct outreach. The goal is to validate if they're genuinely interested and qualify them as potential leads.

Refine and Iterate

Targeting is not a one-time task. As the market evolves, so will your ICP. Regularly revisit and refine your targeting strategy.

Golden Rule #3: "Your most unhappy customers are your greatest source of learning." - Bill Gates, Business @ the Speed of Thought. Use feedback and interactions to continually refine your targeting approach.

In Conclusion,

I leaned back, "Remember, Aanya, targeting is both an art and a science. It requires intuition, but it also heavily relies on data and research. And in an industry as dynamic as healthcare, staying updated and being adaptable is the key."

Aanya nodded, jotting down notes, "Thank you, Dr. Viraj. This gives me a clearer roadmap on how to approach targeting. It's not just about casting a wide net but casting it in the right waters.

Chapter 12: The Sales Lion's Playbook: Proven Techniques for Success

The plane's hum provided a gentle backdrop as Dr. Viraj turned to Aanya with a thoughtful expression. "Aanya, if you had to pick one hobby or activity that you're truly passionate about, what would it be?"

She looked surprised by the sudden shift in the topic but answered, "Well, I've always loved dancing. It's been my escape and my expression."

Dr. Viraj nodded, "And when you dance, do you follow a set routine, or do you improvise?"

Aanya pondered for a moment, "A bit of both, I guess. There's a foundation, but I also let the music guide me."

Smiling, Dr. Viraj said, "Sales, in many ways, is like dancing. There's a foundational playbook, techniques that have been proven to work. But there's also room for improvisation, for letting the 'music' of the situation guide you.

Let's delve into the Sales Lion's Playbook."

1. Understand Your Customer's Pain Points

Before you can offer a solution, you need to understand the problem. In healthcare sales, this could range from a hospital needing more efficient equipment to a doctor seeking better patient management software.

Golden Rule #1: "Seek first to understand, then to be understood." - The 7 Habits of Highly Effective People by

Stephen R. Covey. Always prioritize understanding your customer's needs.

2. Build Genuine Relationships

Sales isn't just about transactions; it's about building trust. Especially in healthcare, where decisions can impact patient lives, trust is paramount.

According to a study by HubSpot, 51% of sales professionals believe that building relationships is crucial for sales success.

3. Offer Value Beyond the Product

Can you provide additional training? Post-sale support? Think of ways you can offer value beyond just the product or service you're selling.

Golden Rule #2: "Give value first." - The Go-Giver by Bob Burg & John David Mann. Always look for ways to offer more than what's expected.

4. Continuously Educate Yourself

The healthcare industry is ever-evolving. New research, new technologies, new regulations. Stay updated to stay relevant.

5. Listen Actively

Active listening involves fully concentrating, understanding, and responding to what the other person is saying. It's not just about hearing the words but understanding the intent.

A survey by LinkedIn found that 42% of salespeople don't feel they have enough information before making a sales call. Active listening can bridge this gap.

6. Handle Objections Gracefully

Objections are a natural part of the sales process. Instead of seeing them as roadblocks, view them as opportunities to provide more clarity and value.

Golden Rule #3: "People don't buy for logical reasons. They buy for emotional reasons." - Zig Ziglar, Secrets of Closing the Sale. Addressing objections often means addressing underlying emotions and concerns.

7. Follow Up, But Don't Pester

Persistence is key in sales, but there's a fine line between being persistent and being a nuisance. Find that balance.

According to InsideSales.com, 50% of sales happen after the 5th contact, but most reps give up after the 2nd attempt.

Dr. Viraj concluded, "The playbook provides the foundation, Aanya. But remember, every customer and every situation are unique. Like in dance, let the rhythm of the situation guide your steps."

Aanya smiled, "That's a perspective I hadn't considered. Thank you, Dr. Viraj. It's like merging the structure of classical dance with the freedom of contemporary."

He chuckled, "Exactly! And that's the dance of sales."

Chapter 13: Overcoming Objections: Handling Resistance with Grace

As the plane continued its journey, Aanya looked at Dr. Viraj with a playful glint in her eyes. "Dr. Viraj, you've shared so much about sales and handling objections in the professional world. But tell me, have you ever faced a challenging objection from your wife? How do you handle situations where opinions are mismatched at home?"

Dr. Viraj laughed heartily, "Ah, Aanya! You've touched upon a topic that's both delicate and intriguing. Handling objections in sales is one thing, but managing differences with a loved one is an art in itself. But you know, the principles are surprisingly similar."

1. Listen Actively

Before responding to an objection, it's crucial to understand it fully. Whether it's a customer's concern or a spouse's disagreement, active listening is the first step.

Fact: According to the Harvard Business Review, active listening can defuse emotional situations, leading to more productive conversations.

2. Empathize and Validate

It's essential to acknowledge the other person's feelings and concerns. By validating their feelings, you're building a bridge of understanding.

Golden Rule #1: "Whenever you feel like criticizing anyone, just remember that all the people in this world haven't had the advantages that you've had." - The Great Gatsby by F. Scott Fitzgerald. Empathy can change the direction of a conversation.

3. Ask Open-Ended Questions

Instead of making statements, ask questions. This not only helps in understanding the root of the objection but also makes the other person feel valued.

Fact: A study by Gong.io found that successful salespeople ask 8-10 questions per meeting, allowing them to handle objections more effectively.

4. Offer Solutions, Not Excuses

Once you understand the objection, focus on finding a solution. Avoid being defensive or making excuses.

Golden Rule #2: "Excuses are the nails used to build a house of failure." - Don Wilder. Focus on solutions to build a foundation of success.

5. Stay Calm and Composed

Emotions can run high during objections. Whether it's a high-stakes sales deal or a disagreement with a loved one, maintaining composure is key.

Fact: According to Psychology Today, staying calm during disagreements can lead to better outcomes and stronger relationships.

6. Agree to Disagree

Sometimes, despite your best efforts, you might not reach a consensus. And that's okay. It's essential to respect differing opinions and find common ground.

Golden Rule #3: "It is the mark of an educated mind to be able to entertain a thought without accepting it." - Aristotle. Respecting differences can lead to mutual respect.

Dr. Viraj smiled, "So, to answer your question, Aanya, yes, I've faced objections and disagreements with my wife. But by applying these principles, we've always found a way to navigate through them gracefully."

Aanya nodded thoughtfully, "It's fascinating how the principles of sales can be applied to personal relationships as well. Life truly is the biggest sales pitch."

Dr. Viraj agreed, "Indeed, Aanya. And the key is to handle every objection, every challenge, with grace and understanding."

Chapter 14: The Power of Presentation: Selling with Confidence

The flight attendants began serving the in-flight meals, placing trays of meticulously arranged food in front of the passengers. Aanya observed the presentation of her meal, the colors, the arrangement, and the attention to detail. She turned to Dr. Viraj with a curious expression, "Dr. Viraj, have you ever been to a restaurant where the presentation of the food left a lasting impression on you? I believe that the way something is presented can significantly influence our perception of it."

Dr. Viraj chuckled, "Ah, Aanya, you've touched upon one of my favorite topics. Presentation is indeed powerful. I remember dining at a restaurant in Paris where the chef presented each dish as if it were a work of art. The experience was unforgettable, not just because of the taste but because of the visual appeal. The same principle applies to sales. The way you present your product or service can make or break a deal."

1. First Impressions Matter

Just as the first look of a dish can set the tone for the dining experience, the initial presentation in sales is crucial. It sets the stage for the entire interaction.

Fact: According to a study by Forbes, it takes just seven seconds for someone to form a first impression.

2. Tailor Your Presentation

Understand your audience and customize your presentation to resonate with them. A one-size-fits-all approach rarely works.

Golden Rule #1: "People don't buy for logical reasons. They buy for emotional reasons." - Zig Ziglar, Secrets of Closing the Sale. Connect emotionally with your audience for a lasting impact.

3. Use Visual Aids

Visual aids can enhance your presentation, making it more engaging and memorable. Whether it's a chart, a graph, or a product demo, visuals can tell a story.

Fact: According to the Visual Teaching Alliance, 65% of people are visual learners.

4. Practice Makes Perfect

Rehearse your presentation multiple times. Familiarity with the content boosts confidence, ensuring a smooth delivery.

Golden Rule #2: "All the great speakers were bad speakers at first." - Ralph Waldo Emerson. Mastery comes with practice.

5. Engage and Interact

A presentation shouldn't be a monologue. Engage your audience, ask questions, and encourage participation. Interaction makes the experience more immersive.

Fact: Interactive presentations are 32% more memorable, 79% more persuasive, and 16% more likely to drive action, according to a study by Prezi.

6. Conclude with a Call to Action

Every presentation should have a clear objective. Conclude with a call to action, guiding your audience on the next steps.

Golden Rule #3: "People often say that motivation doesn't last. Well, neither does bathing - that's why we recommend it daily." - Zig Ziglar. Consistently remind your audience of the action you want them to take.

Dr. Viraj took a bite of his meal, savoring the flavors, "Just as this meal is a blend of taste and presentation, a successful sales pitch is a combination of content and delivery. And remember, Aanya, confidence in your product and in yourself is the key."

Aanya nodded, "It's fascinating how every aspect of life, even something as simple as a meal, can teach us so much about sales and presentation."

Dr. Viraj smiled, "Life is full of lessons, Aanya. We just need to be observant and willing to learn."

Chapter 15: Leveraging Technology: Digital Tools for Modern Sales

As the flight continued, Aanya pulled out her tablet and began browsing through some apps. Dr. Viraj, noticing her comfort with the device, remarked, "You seem quite adept with technology, Aanya. It's impressive to see how seamlessly your generation integrates it into daily life."

Aanya smiled, "Well, I'm a Gen Z, Dr. Viraj. Digital technology is second nature to us. But it's not the same for everyone. My father, for instance, is quite resistant to adopting new technologies. He still prefers his old ways."

Dr. Viraj nodded, "Ah, the classic generational divide. But in sales, especially in today's world, leveraging technology is not just an advantage; it's a necessity."

1. The Generational Classification with Respect to Digital Technology

Baby Boomers (1946-1964): Grew up without digital technology but adapted to it in their later years.

Generation X (1965-1980): Witnessed the dawn of the digital age and were the first to adapt to computers and the internet.

Millennials (1981-1996): The bridge generation that saw the transition from dial-up to broadband and the rise of mobile technology.

Gen Z (1997-2012): Born into a digital world, they are native users of technology and the internet.

Fact: According to Pew Research Center, 98% of Gen Z individuals have a smartphone, and 45% are online "almost constantly."

2. The Power of CRM Systems

Customer Relationship Management (CRM) systems are invaluable tools for sales professionals. They help in tracking interactions, managing leads, and analyzing customer data.

Golden Rule #1: "Adopting a CRM practically increases sales by up to 29%." - Salesforce, State of Sales Report.

3. Social-Media and Sales

Platforms like LinkedIn, Twitter, and Facebook have become essential tools for sales professionals to network, research, and engage with potential clients.

Fact: HubSpot reports that 78% of salespeople using social media outperform their peers.

4. AI and Predictive Analytics

Artificial Intelligence (AI) and predictive analytics can forecast sales trends, identify potential leads, and even automate routine tasks.

Golden Rule #2: "By 2025, AI-related market revenue will reach $190 billion." - John Chambers, Connecting the Dots.

5. Virtual Reality (VR) and Augmented Reality (AR) in Sales

VR and AR can provide immersive product demos, making the sales experience more interactive and engaging.

Fact: According to Deloitte, 88% of mid-market companies are already using some form of virtual or augmented reality as part of their business.

Dr. Viraj leaned in, "Aanya, the resistance your father feels towards technology is natural. Every generation has its comfort zone. But in sales, adapting to the latest tools can make a world of difference."

Aanya pondered, "I understand, Dr. Viraj. It's just hard seeing him struggle sometimes. But I guess it's all about finding a balance between the old and the new."

Golden Rule #3: "Change is the only constant in life. Those who notice the change early and adapt to it are more likely to succeed." - Heraclitus, Fragments.

Key Learnings from Step 3: Strategies for Success

1. Audience Identification: Recognizing and targeting the right audience is the foundation of any successful sales strategy. Tailoring your approach to the specific needs and preferences of your target demographic can significantly increase conversion rates.
2. Research is Crucial: Before approaching potential buyers, thorough research can provide insights into their needs, preferences, and pain points, allowing for a more personalized sales pitch.
3. The Sales Playbook: Having a structured and proven sales strategy can significantly increase the chances of success. Consistency and adaptability in approach are key.

4. Active Listening: One of the most effective sales techniques is active listening. Understanding a client's needs and concerns can help tailor the sales pitch more effectively.
5. Handling Objections: Every salesperson will face objections. The key is to handle them with grace, understanding, and effective counter-arguments without being confrontational.
6. The Power of Storytelling: Narratives can be powerful tools in sales. Sharing personal experiences or success stories can create a connection and build trust.

7. First Impressions Matter: The way a product or service is presented can significantly impact a potential buyer's perception. A well-structured and confident presentation can be the difference between a sale and a missed opportunity.

8. Utilize Visual Aids: Visual aids in presentations, such as charts, graphs, and infographics, can help convey complex information more effectively and leave a lasting impression.

9. Embrace Digital Tools: In the modern sales landscape, leveraging technology, from CRM systems to AI analytics, can provide a competitive edge.

10. Stay Updated: The digital landscape is ever-evolving. Regularly updating oneself with the latest tools and technologies is crucial for modern sales success.

11. Generational Understanding: Recognizing the technological comfort levels of different generations can help in tailoring the sales approach, especially when selling digital products or services.

12. Networking: Building and maintaining a strong professional network can open doors to new opportunities and referrals.

13. Continuous Learning: The sales industry is dynamic. Regular training and upskilling can help sales professionals stay ahead of the curve.

14. Feedback is Gold: Regular feedback, both positive and negative, can provide valuable insights into areas of improvement and potential growth.

15. Adaptability: The ability to adapt to changing circumstances, whether it's a new technology trend or a shift in the market, is a hallmark of a successful sales professional.

Step 4: Team Building and Leadership

In the intricate dance of sales, while individual prowess is commendable, the magic truly unfolds when a team moves in harmony. Step 4 takes you into the world of team dynamics, leadership, and the art of building a winning sales force. After all, even the most skilled salesperson can achieve only so much alone. But with a team? The possibilities are limitless.

Here, we'll explore the nuances of assembling a team that doesn't just work together but thrives together. From hiring the right talent to ensuring they are equipped with the necessary skills, this step is about creating a force to be reckoned with. But a team without a leader is like a ship without a compass. Drawing from Dr. Vijay Viraj's leadership philosophy, we'll delve into what it takes to guide a team with vision, purpose, and integrity.

Motivation is the fuel that drives performance. Through real-life examples and proven strategies, we'll uncover the secrets to keeping a team motivated, inspired, and hungry for success. But it's not all smooth sailing. Conflicts are an inevitable part of any team's journey. How do you navigate these challenges to ensure cohesion and harmony? The answers lie within.

As we journey through this step, we'll also celebrate the milestones, understanding the importance of recognizing and rewarding achievements. After all, a motivated team is a successful team.

Chapter 16: Assembling a Winning Team: Hiring and Training the Best

The plane's hum was a gentle backdrop as Aanya turned to Dr. Viraj, a playful glint in her eyes. "Dr. Viraj, were you ever part of a sports team back in your school or college days?"

Dr. Viraj chuckled, "Ah, you've touched a nostalgic chord! I was the captain of our college cricket team. Those were the days! The thrill of the game, the camaraderie... but most importantly, the lessons on teamwork and leadership. Why do you ask?"

Aanya smiled, "I was part of the basketball team in school. I remember how crucial each player was, and how trust was the foundation of our victories. I'm curious, how does that translate to building a sales team?"

Dr. Viraj nodded, "A brilliant correlation, Aanya. Just like in sports, in sales, you need a team where every member plays their part efficiently. Let's delve into that."

1. Recognizing Talent: The first step in assembling a winning team is identifying the right talent. Look for individuals who not only have the necessary skills but also align with the company's values and culture.

Golden Rule: "Hire character. Train skill." - Peter Schutz

2. Comprehensive Training: Once you've hired the right people, invest in their training. Ensure they understand the product, the market, and the company's sales methodologies. Regular training sessions can keep the team updated with the latest trends and techniques.

copyright@DrVijayViraj

Fact: Companies that invest in comprehensive training programs have 24% higher profit margins than those who spend less on training. (Source: American Society for Training and Development)

3. Building Trust: Trust is the foundation of any successful team. Encourage open communication, recognize achievements, and address concerns promptly.

Golden Rule: "The best way to find out if you can trust somebody is to trust them." - Ernest Hemingway

4. Setting Clear Goals: Every team member should be aware of their individual targets as well as the team's collective goals. This provides direction and purpose.

Fact: Teams with clear goals are 20% more productive than those without. (Source: Harvard Business Review)

5. Continuous Feedback: Regular feedback sessions can help identify areas of improvement. It also provides an opportunity to recognize and reward outstanding performance.

6. Team Building Activities: Engage in activities outside the work environment. This can strengthen bonds and improve team dynamics.

Golden Rule: "Talent wins games, but teamwork and intelligence win championships." - Michael Jordan

7. Adaptability: The sales environment is dynamic. Ensure your team is adaptable to changing circumstances, whether it's a new product launch or a shift in market trends.

Fact: 74% of teams say they're more productive when they embrace adaptability. (Source: Forbes)

8. Celebrate Successes: Recognizing and celebrating achievements, big or small, can boost morale and motivation.

Team Building Formula: Trust + Clear Goals + Open Communication + Recognition = A Winning Sales Team

Dr. Viraj concluded, "Just like in sports, in sales, every team member plays a crucial role. The key is to ensure they have the right training, tools, and motivation to perform at their best."

Aanya looked thoughtful, "It's fascinating how principles from sports can be applied to the professional world. Thank you for sharing, Dr. Viraj."

Chapter 17: The Sales Lion's Leadership Philosophy: Guiding with Vision and Purpose

The gentle hum of the plane's engines had lulled Dr. Viraj into a light nap. His calm demeanor and rhythmic breathing indicated a peaceful slumber. Aanya, however, was restless. Her mind was buzzing with questions, and her innate curiosity was getting the better of her. She hesitated for a moment, then gently shook Dr. Viraj's shoulder.

He stirred, blinking his eyes open, and looked at her with a hint of surprise. "Oh, I must've dozed off," he remarked with a chuckle.

"I'm so sorry, Dr. Viraj," Aanya began, her voice filled with genuine regret. "I know I should've let you rest, but I'm so eager to understand your leadership philosophy. How did you build the 'Sales Lion' brand with such a clear vision and purpose?"

Dr. Viraj smiled warmly, appreciating her enthusiasm. "It's alright, Aanya. Your passion for learning is commendable. Let's dive into it."

1. Visionary Thinking: Every great leader has a vision. It's the north star that guides all actions and decisions. For me, the vision was clear: to revolutionize the healthcare sales training industry and empower individuals with the skills and mindset of a 'Sales Lion'.

Golden Rule: "Good business leaders create a vision, articulate the vision, passionately own the vision, and relentlessly drive it to completion." - Jack Welch

2. Purpose-Driven Actions: A vision without purpose is like a ship without a compass. My purpose was to make a genuine difference in people's lives, helping them achieve their sales goals and, in turn, their life aspirations.

Fact: 89% of employees believe that companies that lead with a strong sense of purpose are more likely to drive success. (Source: Deloitte)

3. Continuous Learning: The world of sales is ever-evolving. I emphasized the importance of continuous learning, both for myself and for those I trained.

Golden Rule: "Leadership and learning are indispensable to each other." - John F. Kennedy

4. Empathy and Understanding: A true leader understands the needs, aspirations, and challenges of their team. I always prioritized building genuine relationships with my trainees and understanding their unique journeys.

Fact: Leaders who demonstrate empathy have teams that are 50% more likely to outperform their targets. (Source: Businessolver)

5. Resilience and Perseverance: The path to success is filled with obstacles. My resilience in the face of challenges and his unwavering perseverance have been instrumental in building the 'Sales Lion' brand.

Golden Rule: "Success is not final, failure is not fatal: It is the courage to continue that count." - Winston Churchill

The 7 Principles Every Sales Leader Must Embody:

1. Integrity: Always be honest and transparent in your dealings.

2. Adaptability: Be ready to pivot and adapt to changing market dynamics.

3. Collaboration: Foster a culture of teamwork and collective growth.

4. Innovation: Encourage new ideas and out-of-the-box thinking.

5. Accountability: Take responsibility for your actions and decisions.

6. Passion: Be genuinely passionate about your product, service, and team.

7. Customer-Centricity: Always prioritize the needs and feedback of your customers.

Dr. Viraj concluded, "Building the 'Sales Lion' brand wasn't just about imparting sales techniques. It was about instilling a mindset, a philosophy. It's about leading with vision, purpose, and a set of core principles."

Aanya nodded, absorbing every word. "Thank you, Dr. Viraj. Your journey and philosophy are truly inspiring."

He smiled, "It's been a pleasure sharing it with you, Aanya

Chapter 18: Motivating Your Team: Inspiring Peak Performance

The plane's gentle hum provided a comforting backdrop as Aanya and Dr. Viraj continued their conversation. Aanya, with a hint of hesitation in her voice, asked, "Dr. Viraj, have you ever felt demotivated or depressed during your journey? How did you bounce back from such phases?"

Dr. Viraj took a deep breath, his eyes reflecting a distant memory. "Aanya, like everyone, I've had my moments of doubt and despair. There was a time when I faced a series of setbacks, both personally and professionally. It felt like the universe was conspiring against me."

Golden Rule: "Our greatest glory is not in never falling, but in rising every time we fall." - Confucius

The Downward Spiral: I recounted a phase where I lost a significant client, faced challenges in my personal relationships, and grappled with health issues. The cumulative effect of these events took a toll on my mental well-being.

Fact: According to a study by Gallup, 67% of employees are not engaged at work, and 18% are actively disengaged, which can lead to decreased productivity and morale. (Source: Gallup)

The Bounce Back: I emphasized the importance of self-awareness and seeking support. "I reached out to mentors, read motivational books, and most importantly, took time for self-reflection. I realized that motivation is an internal force.

External factors can influence it, but the true drive comes from within."

Golden Rule: "People often say that motivation doesn't last. Well, neither does bathing - that's why we recommend it daily."
- Zig Ziglar

Relating to Sales Leadership: Drawing parallels to sales leadership, I highlighted, "Just as I needed motivation during my low phase, sales teams need constant motivation to perform at their peak. The challenges they face - rejections, competition, market fluctuations - can be demoralizing. As a leader, it's your responsibility to inspire and uplift them."

Fact: Companies with engaged employees outperform those without by 202%. (Source: Business2Community)

10 Tips for Sales Leaders to Inspire Peak Performance:

1. Set Clear Goals: Define achievable targets and communicate them effectively.

2. Recognize Achievements: Celebrate small wins to boost morale.

3. Provide Continuous Training: Equip your team with the latest skills and knowledge.

4. Foster a Positive Work Environment: Encourage open communication and camaraderie.

5. Offer Constructive Feedback: Help team members learn from their mistakes.

6. Empower Decision Making: Trust your team and give them autonomy.

7. Provide Growth Opportunities: Show a clear path for career advancement.

8. Lead by Example: Be a role model in attitude and work ethic.

9. Encourage Work-Life Balance: Ensure your team has time to recharge.

10. Stay Updated: Keep abreast of industry trends and share insights.

I concluded, "Motivation is the fuel that drives us. As leaders, we must ensure that this fuel is constantly replenished, not just for ourselves but for our teams as well."

Aanya, deeply engrossed in the conversation, nodded in agreement. "Thank you, Dr. Viraj. Your insights are invaluable."

Chapter 19: Handling Team Conflicts: Navigating Challenges for Cohesion

As the flight continued its journey, I noticed Aanya gazing at her phone screen, which displayed a picture of her parents. The smile on their faces contrasted with the sadness in her eyes. I gently inquired, "Aanya, is everything okay?"

She hesitated for a moment before sharing, "My parents have been having conflicts lately. It's hard to see them argue over trivial matters."

I nodded understandingly. "Family is like a team, Aanya. Just as conflicts arise in families, they also emerge in sales teams. The key is to navigate these challenges effectively to maintain cohesion."

Golden Rule: "The strength of the team is each individual member. The strength of each member is the team." - Phil Jackson

Fact: According to CPP Inc., U.S. employees spend 2.8 hours per week dealing with conflict, which amounts to approximately $359 billion in paid hours. (Source: CPP Global Human Capital Report)

Understanding the Root Cause: The first step in handling conflict is understanding its root cause. Whether it's a difference in opinion, competition for resources, or personal issues, identifying the underlying reason is crucial.

Golden Rule: "Whenever you're in conflict with someone, there is one factor that can make the difference between damaging your relationship and deepening it. That factor is attitude." - William James

Effective Communication: Open and honest communication is the cornerstone of resolving conflicts. Encouraging team members to express their concerns and feelings can pave the way for understanding and resolution.

Fact: 70% of employees believe that open communication can mitigate workplace conflict. (Source: MyHub Intranet Solutions)

Mediation and Intervention: Sometimes, conflicts escalate to a point where intervention is necessary. As a leader, stepping in to mediate and provide solutions can prevent further escalation.

Building a Cohesive Environment: Promoting team-building activities, fostering a culture of respect, and setting clear expectations can minimize conflicts. A cohesive environment where team members feel valued and heard can significantly reduce disagreements.

Golden Rule: "Peace is not the absence of conflict, but the ability to cope with it." - Dorothy Thomas

Lessons from Family Conflicts: Drawing parallels from Aanya 's situation, I shared, "Just as in families, conflicts in sales teams arise from differences. But these differences can be harnessed positively. Diverse perspectives can lead to innovative solutions. The key is to channelize disagreements constructively."

Aanya looked thoughtful. "I never saw it that way. Thank you for providing a fresh perspective."

I smiled, "Always remember, Aanya, conflicts are inevitable, but how we handle them defines our relationships, be it in families or sales teams."

Chapter 20: Celebrating Success: Recognizing and Rewarding Achievements

The hum of the airplane engines was momentarily overshadowed by the cabin crew's announcement. "Ladies and gentlemen, we have a special group onboard celebrating a significant milestone. We'll be cutting a cake in their honor shortly."

Aanya looked a bit puzzled and perhaps even slightly uncomfortable. "Isn't that a bit over-the-top, celebrating on a plane?"

I chuckled, "Aanya, celebrations, no matter how big or small, play a crucial role, especially in sales. Let me explain."

Golden Rule: "Success is sweet: the sweeter if long delayed and attained through manifold struggles and defeats." - A. Branson Alcott

Fact: According to a study by the Incentive Research Foundation, well-designed incentive programs can increase performance by anywhere from 25% to 44%. (Source: Incentive Research Foundation)

The Power of Recognition: Recognizing achievements, even the smallest ones, can boost morale and motivation. It's not just about the monetary rewards; it's about acknowledging hard work and dedication.

Golden Rule: "People work for money but go the extra mile for recognition, praise, and rewards." - Dale Carnegie

Case Study: Unicorn Denmart Ltd.

During my tenure as the Manager of Digital Sales at Unicorn Denmart Ltd., we faced a challenging quarter. Sales were dwindling, and the team's morale was at an all-time low. I introduced a 'Celebration Friday' initiative. Every small achievement, every target met, was celebrated. It wasn't always grand, sometimes just a cake or a team lunch. But the impact was profound.

By the end of the quarter, not only had we met our sales target, but we exceeded it by 50%. The team was more cohesive, motivated, and driven. The simple act of celebrating our successes, no matter how minor, created a ripple effect of positivity and productivity.

Fact: Companies that invest in employee recognition are 12 times more likely to generate strong business results. (Source: Bersin by Deloitte)

The Importance of Personal Touch: Personalized rewards, tailored to the individual's preferences, can have a more significant impact than generic ones. It shows that the company values and understands its employees.

Golden Rule: "People don't care how much you know until they know how much you care." - Theodore Roosevelt

I turned to Aanya, "Celebrations are not just about the act itself but the sentiment behind it. It's about valuing effort, fostering a positive environment, and driving motivation."

Aanya 's eyes sparkled with understanding, "I see your point. It's the little things, the gestures that make a difference."

I nodded, "Exactly. In sales, as in life, it's essential to pause, acknowledge, and celebrate the journey."

Key Learnings from Step 4: Team Building and Leadership

1. Hiring the Right Fit: It's essential to hire individuals who align with the company's values and vision. Skills can be taught, but attitude and cultural fit are intrinsic.
2. Continuous Training: Regular training sessions ensure that the team is updated with the latest industry trends, product knowledge, and sales techniques.
3. Visionary Leadership: A leader should have a clear vision and purpose. This not only guides the team but also inspires them to align their individual goals with the company's objectives.
4. Golden Rule of Leadership: "Leadership is not about being in charge. It's about taking care of those in your charge." - Simon Sinek
5. Intrinsic Motivation: While external rewards are essential, tapping into an individual's intrinsic motivation leads to sustained peak performance.
6. Conflict Resolution: Conflicts are inevitable in a team setting. Effective leaders address issues head-on, ensuring they're resolved amicably and constructively.
7. Golden Rule of Conflict: "Peace is not the absence of conflict, but the ability to handle conflict by peaceful means." - Ronald Reagan
8. Celebration and Recognition: Regularly acknowledging and celebrating achievements, big or small, boosts morale and fosters a positive work environment.
9. Personalized Rewards: Tailoring rewards to individual preferences shows that the company values and

understands its employees, leading to increased loyalty and motivation.

10. Golden Rule of Recognition: "People work for money but go the extra mile for recognition, praise, and rewards." - Dale Carnegie

11. Open Communication: Fostering an environment where team members feel comfortable sharing their ideas, concerns, and feedback is crucial for team cohesion and innovation.

12. Lead by Example: Leaders should embody the values and work ethic they expect from their team. This not only sets the standard but also builds trust and respect.

13. Adaptability: In the ever-evolving world of sales, adaptability is key. Leaders should be open to change and encourage their team to be flexible and receptive to new strategies and technologies.

14. Feedback Loop: Regular feedback sessions help in identifying areas of improvement and also in acknowledging the efforts of team members.

15. Team Dynamics: Understanding the strengths and weaknesses of each team member and leveraging them effectively ensures a harmonious and productive team environment.

Step 5: Analyzing the Competition

The world of sales is akin to a vast ocean, teeming with diverse marine life, where every entity is vying for its own space, survival, and dominance. In this vast ocean, understanding the movements and strategies of other marine creatures is crucial for one's own survival and growth. Step 5 delves deep into this oceanic world of competition, guiding you through the currents and tides of the competitive landscape in healthcare sales.

Every salesperson, no matter how skilled, operates within a larger ecosystem. This ecosystem is shaped by competitors, their strategies, their successes, and their failures. Recognizing and understanding this competition is not just about staying ahead; it's about carving out a unique space for oneself and one's products.

In this step, we'll embark on a journey to dissect the competitive landscape, identifying key players, understanding their strategies, and learning how to position oneself effectively. Drawing from Dr. Vijay Viraj's experiences, we'll uncover the tactics and strategies that have allowed him to stand out in a crowded field and outperform major competitors.

But it's not just about understanding the competition; it's about learning from them. Innovation, adaptation, and strategic positioning become the pillars of success in a competitive market. Through real-life case studies, we'll explore how to adapt and innovate based on competitive insights.

Chapter 21: Understanding the Competitive Landscape: Who's Who in Healthcare Sales

As the plane continued its journey, Aanya flipped through the in-flight magazine. Her eyes landed on an advertisement for a premium coffee brand. The ad was sleek, with a tagline that read, "Experience luxury in every sip." She turned to me and remarked, "You know, Dr. Vijay, this brand has become so popular recently. Just a year ago, they were nowhere on the radar, and now they're everywhere. How do brands manage to stand out in such a competitive market?"

I smiled, taking a moment to sip my own coffee. "It's all about understanding the competitive landscape, Aanya. Just like in the coffee industry, the healthcare sales sector is teeming with players, each vying for a piece of the pie. To succeed, one must know who the key players are, what they offer, and how to differentiate oneself."

1. The Major Players in Healthcare Sales: The healthcare sales industry is vast, comprising various segments like pharmaceuticals, medical devices, surgical equipment, and digital health solutions. Key players include:

Pharmaceutical Companies: Giants like Pfizer, Novartis, and Roche dominate the market, but there are numerous smaller firms making significant inroads.

Medical-Dental Device Manufacturers/ Suppliers: Companies like Medtronic, Boston Scientific, and Johnson & Johnson are at the forefront, offering innovative solutions for patient care. Not to forget, Unicorn Denmart Ltd, which has made a significant impact in the dental equipment sector, providing state-of-the-art solutions and maintaining a strong presence in the market.

Digital Health Solutions: With the rise of telemedicine and health apps, startups and tech giants alike are entering this space.

2. Emerging Trends: The healthcare sales landscape is continually evolving. Recent trends include a shift towards personalized medicine, increased focus on patient-centric care, and the integration of AI and machine learning in diagnostics and treatment.

Golden Rule: "Know your competition as well as you know yourself. Only then can you strategize effectively." - Sun Tzu, The Art of War

3. Market Share and Growth: In 2022, the global healthcare market was valued at approximately $8.45 trillion, with a projected CAGR of 8.9% over the next five years. The pharmaceutical segment alone accounted for 45% of this value.

4. Niche Players: While the giants dominate the headlines, niche players cater to specific segments, offering specialized solutions. For instance, in the orthodontic space, companies like 32 Watts Clear Aligners have carved a niche for themselves.

Golden Rule: "In a crowded marketplace, fitting in is failing. In a busy marketplace, not standing out is the same as being invisible." - Seth Godin, Purple Cow

5. The Importance of Differentiation: To stand out, companies must offer something unique, be it in terms of product quality, customer service, or innovative solutions. It's not just about having a superior product but also about effectively communicating its benefits to the target audience.

Golden Rule: "Differentiate or die." - Jack Trout, Differentiate or Die

I concluded, "Just like the coffee brand you noticed, Aanya, companies in the healthcare sales sector must constantly innovate, adapt, and differentiate themselves to stay ahead. It's a dynamic field, and only those who truly understand the competitive landscape can hope to thrive."

Aanya looked thoughtful. "It's fascinating how principles from one industry can apply to another. Whether it's coffee or healthcare, the fundamentals remain the same."

I nodded in agreement. "Indeed, Aanya. Business, at its core, is about understanding the market, the competition, and most importantly, the customer."

Chapter 22: The Sales Lion's Competitive Edge: Standing Out in a Crowded Field

As the plane soared above the clouds, Aanya looked out of the window, lost in thought. After a few moments, she turned to me with a curious expression. "You know, in a vast ocean of salespeople, what makes someone like you stand out? What's your secret sauce?"

I chuckled, "Ah, the million-dollar question! Well, Aanya, it's not just one thing. It's a combination of factors that give someone the competitive edge."

1. Deep Industry Knowledge: The first and foremost factor is having an in-depth understanding of the industry. It's not just about knowing your product but understanding the entire ecosystem. For instance, in healthcare sales, it's crucial to know the latest medical advancements, regulatory changes, and patient preferences.

Golden Rule: "Knowledge is a competitive advantage." - Robert T. Kiyosaki, Rich Dad Poor Dad

2. Building Genuine Relationships: Sales is not just about transactions; it's about building relationships. It's about understanding the needs of your clients and offering solutions that truly benefit them. Over the years, I've realized that genuine concern and empathy go a long way in establishing trust.

Golden Rule: "People don't care how much you know until they know how much you care." - Theodore Roosevelt

3. Continuous Learning and Adaptability: The sales landscape is ever-evolving. What worked five years ago might not work today. I've always believed in continuous learning. Whether it's attending workshops, reading books, or engaging in online courses, staying updated is the key.

Fact: According to LinkedIn, 94% of employees would stay at a company longer if it invested in their learning and development.

4. Leveraging Technology: In today's digital age, technology plays a pivotal role in sales. Whether it's using CRM tools to manage leads or AI-driven analytics to understand customer behavior, technology provides that extra edge.

Golden Rule: "Embrace change to stay ahead. Use technology as an enabler, not just a tool." - Brian Halligan, HubSpot

5. Authenticity and Integrity: In the long run, authenticity and integrity matter the most. People can see through pretense. Being genuine and upholding your values, even when it's challenging, sets you apart.

Fact: A survey by Boston Consulting Group found that authenticity is one of the top qualities that employees value in their leaders.

I paused, taking a sip of my drink. "Aanya, the essence of standing out in a crowded field is not just about being better but being different. It's about finding that unique value proposition that resonates with your audience."

Aanya nodded, absorbing the information. "So, it's a mix of knowledge, relationships, adaptability, technology, and authenticity. But tell me, how do you ensure that you don't get lost in the crowd?"

I smiled, "By constantly asking myself: 'What value am I bringing to the table? How am I making a difference?' And by always striving to be the best version of myself."

Aanya seemed impressed. "That's a powerful approach. It's no wonder you're the Sales Lion!"

Chapter 23: Learning from Competitors: Adapting and Innovating

"We are reaching New York in next 40 minutes", The captain's announcement seemed to jolt Aanya from her reflective state. She looked at me, a hint of urgency in her eyes. "We don't have much time left, but I have so many questions! Before we land, can you tell me about how you view competition? How do you learn from them?"

I smiled reassuringly, "Competition, Aanya, is one of the best teachers you can have. Let me explain."

1. A Mirror to Self-Reflection: Competitors often serve as a mirror, reflecting back our strengths and weaknesses. By analyzing what they're doing right and where they're faltering, we can introspect on our own strategies and make necessary adjustments.

Golden Rule: "Business is like war in one respect. If its grand strategy is correct, any number of tactical errors can be made and yet the enterprise proves successful." - Robert A. Waterman Jr., In Search of Excellence

Fact: According to a study by McKinsey, companies that prioritize innovation in their strategies tend to outperform their peers by 2.3 times in terms of profit.

2. Source of Inspiration: While it's essential not to copy competitors, they can be a great source of inspiration. Observing their strategies, campaigns, and customer interactions can spark new ideas and approaches for our own business.

Golden Rule: "Innovation distinguishes between a leader and a follower." - Steve Jobs

3. Identifying Market Gaps: Competitors can help identify gaps in the market. If there's a service they aren't offering or a demographic they aren't targeting, it presents an opportunity for us to step in and fill that void.

Fact: 85% of B2B marketers say that lead generation is their most important content marketing goal, yet many miss out on targeting niche markets.

4. Pushing Boundaries: A competitive market pushes businesses to constantly evolve and improve. It's a driving force that ensures we don't become complacent and always strive for excellence.

Golden Rule: "The competitor to be feared is one who never bothers about you at all, but goes on making his own business better all the time." - Henry Ford

I leaned in, "Aanya, the key is not to be threatened by competition but to embrace it. It's about adapting their best practices, innovating on them, and making them your own."

Aanya looked thoughtful, "So, it's like a continuous cycle of learning, adapting, and evolving."

"Exactly," I replied. "And remember, while it's essential to keep an eye on the competition, it's equally important to stay true to your brand's vision and values."

As the plane began its descent, Aanya 's face lit up with gratitude. "Thank you for sharing so much wisdom. This journey has been more enlightening than I ever imagined."

I nodded, "It was my pleasure. Remember, every experience, every interaction, is an opportunity to learn and grow. Embrace it.

Chapter 24: Strategic Positioning: Carving Out Your Niche

The plane's descent was smooth, and the city lights of New York began to shimmer below. Aanya, looking out of the window, seemed lost in thought. After a moment, she turned to me, her eyes curious. "In such a vast market, with so many players, how do you ensure you stand out? How do you find your unique space?"

I smiled, "Ah, the art of strategic positioning. Let me break it down for you."

1. Understanding Your Unique Value Proposition (UVP): Every business has something unique to offer. It's essential to identify and communicate this UVP clearly to your target audience. It's what sets you apart from the crowd.

Golden Rule: "If you don't have a competitive advantage, don't compete." - Jack Welch

Fact: According to a study by Gallup, companies that effectively communicate their UVP can achieve up to a 3x higher customer retention rate.

2. Know Your Audience: It's crucial to understand who your products or services are for. By having a clear picture of your target audience, you can tailor your offerings and messaging to resonate with them deeply.

Aanya interjected, "Like how luxury brands target a specific segment of the population?"

"Exactly," I replied. "They've carved a niche for themselves by understanding their audience's aspirations and desires."

Golden Rule: "You can't be everything to everyone, but you can be something great for someone." - Derek Halpern

3. Consistency is Key: Once you've identified your niche, it's essential to maintain consistency in your messaging, branding, and customer experience. This builds trust and reinforces your position in the market.

Fact: Consistent branding across all channels can increase revenue by up to 23%.

Aanya looked thoughtful, "So, it's about finding that sweet spot where your strengths meet market demand?"

I nodded, "Precisely. And once you've found it, you need to own it, nurture it, and protect it."

She hesitated for a moment, then asked, "On a personal note, how did you find your niche in life? Was there a defining moment?"

I chuckled, "Life is a series of defining moments, Aanya. For me, it was when I realized that my passion for sales could be combined with my desire to teach and mentor. That's when I carved my niche as a sales trainer."

Aanya smiled, "And what about outside of work? Any personal niches?"

I thought for a moment, "Well, I've always had a passion for photography. It's my way of capturing moments, carving out my little niche in the vast canvas of time."

She laughed, "That's beautifully put. I guess we all have our niches, in work and life. It's just about finding them."

I nodded, "And once you do, it's about making sure you shine the brightest in that space."

As the plane touched down, the conversation seemed to have come full circle. From the vastness of the market to the niches in our personal lives, it was a journey of discovery and understanding.

Chapter 25: Case Study: Outperforming a Major Competitor

As we disembarked from the plane and made our way towards the luggage carousel, the hum of the airport surrounded us. Aanya, pulling her carry-on behind her, turned to me with a thoughtful expression. "You've shared so much about sales strategies and positioning, but I'm curious. Have you ever faced a situation where you had to outperform a major competitor?"

I grinned, recalling a particular instance. "Ah, let me tell you about the time when I was up against Goliath in the market."

The Backdrop: A few years back, I was working with a company that was relatively new in the dental equipment sector. We were up against a giant, a brand that had dominated the market for decades. On paper, it seemed like an impossible task.

Golden Rule: "Opportunities don't happen. You create them." - Chris Grosser

The Challenge: Our competitor had a more extensive product range, a bigger marketing budget, and a well-established brand presence. We needed to increase our market share by 20% within a year.

Fact: According to Harvard Business Review, 85% of 30,000 new product launches in the US fail because of poor market segmentation.

The Strategy:

1. Deep Market Segmentation: We dived deep into market research, identifying niches within the dental sector that were underserved.

Tailored Solutions: Instead of offering generic products, we customized our solutions to cater to these niches.

2. Aggressive Training: We invested heavily in training our sales team, ensuring they had in-depth product knowledge and understood the unique selling points.
3. Building Relationships: We focused on building strong relationships with key decision-makers in the dental industry, organizing workshops, and offering value-added services.

Golden Rule: "It's not about having the right opportunities. It's about handling the opportunities right." - Mark Hunter

The Outcome: Within ten months, not only did we achieve our target of a 20% market share increase, but we also managed to get some of the competitor's key clients on board.

Fact: A study by Bain & Company indicates that increasing customer retention rates by 5% can increase profits by up to 95%.

As we waited for our luggage, Aanya looked impressed. "That's quite a feat! It just goes to show that with the right strategy, even the underdog can come out on top."

I nodded, "It's all about understanding the market, playing to your strengths, and never underestimating the power of relationships."

Golden Rule: "The competitor to be feared is one who never bothers about you at all but goes on making his own business better all the time." - Henry Ford

As our bags finally arrived, Aanya turned to me, "Before we part ways, I'd love to stay in touch. Here's my address." She handed me a card with her details: Aanya Sharma, 1234 Elm Street, New York, NY 10001.

I smiled, taking out my card, "And here's where I'll be staying for the next week." The card read: Dr. Vijay Viraj, The Grand Manhattan Hotel, 5678 Broadway, New York, NY 10019.

She raised an eyebrow, "So, what's your plan for the next seven days in New York?"

I chuckled, "Well, I'm here for a special mentoring program. This time, I'm on the other side of the table, as a mentee. Always learning, always growing."

Aanya smiled, "That's the spirit! Maybe we can catch up for coffee sometime during your stay."

I nodded, "I'd like that. Until then, take care, Aanya."

With that, we parted ways, each heading in our direction, but with the promise of another insightful conversation in the near future.

Golden Rules and Key Learnings from Step 5: Analyzing the Competition

1. Know Your Landscape: Understanding the competitive landscape is crucial. Recognize the major players, their strengths, and their weaknesses. This knowledge is the foundation for strategic planning.
2. Golden Rule: "Opportunities don't happen. You create them." - Chris Grosser
3. Learning: Actively seek and create opportunities rather than waiting for them to come to you.
4. Unique Selling Proposition (USP): In a crowded market, your USP is what sets you apart. It's essential to identify and communicate what makes your product or service unique.
5. Golden Rule: "It's not about having the right opportunities. It's about handling the opportunities right." - Mark Hunter
6. Learning: Success isn't just about identifying opportunities but leveraging them effectively.
7. Adapt and Innovate: Observing competitors isn't about imitation but learning. Adapt their successful strategies and innovate to make them even better.

8. Golden Rule: "The competitor to be feared is one who never bothers about you at all but goes on making his own business better all the time." - Henry Ford

9. Learning: Focus on improving your business continuously rather than getting distracted by competitors.

10. Strategic Positioning: Carving out a niche is about understanding where you fit in the market and positioning yourself effectively to cater to that segment.

11. Golden Rule: "Differentiate or die." - Jack Trout

12. Learning: In a competitive market, differentiation is key. Offer something distinct or risk becoming irrelevant.

13. Case Studies are Gold: Real-life examples, like outperforming a major competitor, provide tangible evidence of strategies in action and their results.

14. Golden Rule: "Know thy self, know thy enemy. A thousand battles, a thousand victories." - Sun Tzu

15. Learning: Deep knowledge of your own strengths and weaknesses, as well as those of your competitors, leads to consistent victories.

16. Continuous Learning: The market, competitors, and strategies evolve. Stay updated and be ready to pivot when necessary.

17. Golden Rule: "What gets measured gets managed." - Peter Drucker

18. Learning: Regularly analyze and measure your strategies against competitors to ensure optimal performance.

19. Celebrate Successes: Recognizing and celebrating achievements, both big and small, boosts morale and motivation.

20. Golden Rule: "Your most unhappy customers are your greatest source of learning." - Bill Gates

21. Learning: Feedback, even negative, is valuable. It offers insights into areas of improvement.

22. Stay Curious: Always be inquisitive about the market, competitors, and emerging trends. Curiosity fuels innovation and keeps you ahead of the curve.

23. These golden rules and learnings serve as guiding principles in the competitive world of healthcare sales. By internalizing and applying them, sales professionals can navigate challenges and seize opportunities effectively.

Step 6: Operational Excellence

In the intricate dance of sales, while the spotlight often shines brightest on the front-end – the deals, the negotiations, the relationships – it's the backstage, the operations, that ensures the dance goes on seamlessly. Step 6 pulls back the curtain on this critical aspect of sales: operational excellence.

Imagine a well-oiled machine, where every cog, every gear, every component works in perfect harmony. This is the vision for sales operations at its peak. But achieving this state of operational excellence is no small feat. It requires meticulous planning, streamlined processes, and a commitment to continuous improvement.

In this step, we'll explore the nuts and bolts of sales operations. From streamlining sales processes to leveraging data for informed decision-making, we'll delve into the strategies and best practices that ensure efficiency and effectiveness in operations. Drawing from Dr. Vijay Viraj's vast experience, we'll uncover the operational strategies that have underpinned his success in the world of healthcare sales.

But operational excellence isn't just about processes and systems; it's about people. Ensuring that feedback loops are in place, that there's a culture of continuous improvement, and that every member of the team is aligned with the operational vision is crucial.

Step 6 is a journey into the heart of sales operations. It's about understanding the importance of the backstage, the behind-the-scenes efforts that ensure the spotlight shines bright. In this step, we'll learn that in the world of sales, operational excellence isn't just a goal; it's a necessity. Welcome to Step 6.

Chapter 26: Streamlining Sales Processes: Efficiency and Effectiveness

The sun was just beginning to cast its golden hue over the city when I entered the hotel's breakfast area. To my surprise, I spotted Aanya already seated at a table, engrossed in a book. As I approached, she looked up and greeted me with a bright smile.

"Good morning, Dr. Vijay! I hope you don't mind me joining you for breakfast," she said, her enthusiasm evident.

I chuckled, "Not at all, Aanya . In fact, I'm impressed by your dedication. It's not every day that someone is so eager to learn that they show up at my breakfast table."

She blushed slightly, "I was restless last night, thinking about all the insights you shared. Plus, I wanted to give you a taste of this special homemade dish my mom prepared." She pointed to a container on the table.

Curious, I asked, "What's the dish? It smells delightful."

"It's a traditional recipe passed down in my family. It requires specific ingredients, precise timing, and a particular sequence of steps to get it just right," she explained.

I smiled, realizing the parallel she was drawing. "Much like a streamlined sales process, isn't it? Specific steps, precise timing, and the right ingredients or tools to ensure efficiency and effectiveness."

Aanya 's eyes lit up, "Exactly! So, how do we ensure that our sales processes are both efficient and effective?"

Golden Rule: "Efficiency is doing things right; effectiveness is doing the right things." - Peter Drucker

Learning: It's not just about doing tasks quickly, but ensuring those tasks align with the end goal.

I began, "Streamlining sales processes is crucial for any organization. It's about eliminating redundancies, automating repetitive tasks, and ensuring that every step adds value to the sales journey."

1. Audit Existing Processes: Start by mapping out the current sales process. Identify bottlenecks, redundant steps, and areas of improvement. According to a study by Salesforce, 68% of companies have not identified or attempted to measure a sales funnel, leading to inefficiencies.

2. Implement Sales Automation Tools: Tools like CRM systems can automate data entry, lead tracking, and follow-ups. This not only saves time but ensures no lead is overlooked.

3. Continuous Training: The sales landscape is ever-evolving. Regular training ensures that the sales team is updated with the latest techniques and tools. A report by LinkedIn showed that continuous learning makes salespeople 50% more likely to achieve sales quotas.

Golden Rule: "Simplicity is the ultimate sophistication." - Leonardo da Vinci

Learning: A streamlined process is simple and devoid of unnecessary complexities, making it more effective.

Aanya took a bite of her dish and said, "Just like this dish, it's about getting the sequence right, isn't it?"

"Absolutely," I replied. "And sometimes, it's about experimenting. Maybe a new tool or a different approach could enhance the process. But remember, the goal is always to serve the customer in the best possible way."

4. Regular Feedback: Encourage feedback from the sales team. They are on the frontline and can provide insights into what's working and what's not.

5. Monitor and Measure: Use metrics to gauge the effectiveness of the sales process. Regularly review these metrics to ensure alignment with organizational goals.

Golden Rule: "What gets measured gets improved." - Robin S. Sharma

Learning: Regular monitoring and measurement lead to continuous improvement in the sales process.

As we were having our breakfast and instructed waiter for a coffee, Aanya seemed deep in thought. "Thank you, Dr. Vijay. This has been enlightening. Streamlining isn't just about speed; it's about direction and purpose."

I nodded, "Exactly. And just like your dish, when done right, the results are delightful."

We both shared a laugh, realizing that sales, much like cooking, is an art and science combined.

Chapter 27: The Role of Data: Informed Decision-Making

The aroma of freshly brewed coffee wafted through the air as Aanya and I continued our breakfast conversation. I noticed her meticulously arranging her plate, separating the fruits from the pastries, and the savory items on the other side.

"Organizing your plate much like data, aren't you?" I teased.

She laughed, "Well, I like to know what I'm eating. It helps me make informed choices about my diet."

I raised an eyebrow, intrigued by her response. "That's an interesting perspective. Just as you use visual data on your plate to make decisions, businesses use data to make informed decisions in sales. Data is the new oil, after all."

Golden Rule: "Without big data, you are blind and deaf in the middle of a freeway." - Geoffrey Moore

Learning: Data provides clarity and direction in the chaotic world of sales.

Aanya looked thoughtful, "But how does one sift through the vast amounts of data available?"

1. Data Collection: The first step is to gather relevant data. This could be from CRM systems, sales reports, customer feedback, and market research. According to Forbes, 79% of executives believe that failing to embrace big data will lead to bankruptcy.

2. Data Analysis: Once collected, data needs to be analyzed to extract meaningful insights. This involves looking for patterns, trends, and anomalies. A study by McKinsey found that companies that leverage customer behavioral insights outperform peers by 85% in sales growth.

Golden Rule: "Data is the sword of the 21st century; those who wield it well are the Samurai." - Jonathan Rosenberg

Learning: Mastery over data gives businesses a competitive edge.

I took a sip of my coffee and asked, "Aanya, have you ever been to a buffet where there are so many options that you don't know where to start?"

She nodded, "Yes, it's overwhelming."

"That's how businesses feel without proper data management. They have a wealth of information but don't know how to utilize it effectively."

3. Data Visualization: Tools like dashboards and graphs help in presenting data in an easily digestible format. It aids in quick decision-making. Gartner reports that by 2025, data storytelling will be the most widespread way of using data in organizations.

4. Actionable Insights: Data in itself is just numbers. The real value lies in the insights derived from it and how they are acted upon. For instance, if data shows a particular product is not selling in a region, strategies can be tweaked accordingly.

Golden Rule: "It's not about how much data you have. It's what you do with it." - Jay Baer

Learning: The real power of data lies in its application.

I leaned forward, "Aanya, think of your favorite dish. Now, imagine if you had data on its nutritional value, popularity, and the best ingredients to use. Wouldn't that enhance your experience?"

She smiled, "Absolutely! It would make me appreciate it even more."

"That's the power of data in sales. It enhances the experience, not just for businesses but for customers too."

As we wrapped up our meal, I posed a thought-provoking question, "If data were a dish, what would it be?"

Aanya pondered for a moment, "A salad. A mix of various ingredients, each adding value, but when combined, it gives a complete picture."

I nodded in agreement, "Precisely. And just like a salad, data is best served fresh and well-mixed."

Chapter 28: Supply Chain Management: Ensuring Product Availability

As we left the breakfast area, Aanya gestured towards the long, ornate corridor of the hotel. "Dr. Vijay, have you ever thought about how everything in this hotel, from the food we just ate to the sheets on the beds, is always available when we need it?"

I smiled, recognizing the direction she was taking the conversation. "You're talking about supply chain management, aren't you?"

She nodded, "Exactly! Just like this hotel ensures everything is in place for its guests, businesses, especially in healthcare sales, must ensure their products are always available for their customers."

Golden Rule: "The most important thing is to forecast where customers are moving, and be in front of them." - Philip Kotler

Learning: Anticipating customer needs is crucial in supply chain management.

1. Demand Forecasting: This involves predicting future product demand to ensure stock availability. According to a study by Aberdeen Group, companies with accurate forecasts are 10% more likely to achieve their revenue goals.

2. Inventory Management: It's a delicate balance between overstocking and stockouts. Both can be costly. The Harvard Business Review states that U.S. retailers lose $634.1 billion annually due to stockouts and $471.9 billion due to overstocks.

Golden Rule: "Inventory is money sitting around in another form." - Rhonda Abrams

Learning: Efficient inventory management translates to better cash flow.

As we walked, I pointed to the housekeeping carts, "See those? They ensure that every room has fresh towels and amenities. That's a simple example of inventory management."

Aanya looked thoughtful, "So, it's all interconnected? The suppliers, the hotel, and the guests?"

3. Supplier Relationships: Building strong relationships with suppliers ensures a consistent and quality supply. A Deloitte survey found that 79% of companies with high-performing supply chains achieve revenue growth greater than the average within their industries.

4. Logistics and Distribution: This involves the transportation of products from manufacturers to end-users. Efficient logistics can reduce costs and improve customer satisfaction. According to PwC, transportation costs can account for 50% of total logistics costs, emphasizing the need for optimization.

Golden Rule: "Supply chain is like nature; it is all around us." - Dave Waters

Learning: Every touchpoint in a business is part of the supply chain.

I paused as we reached my room. "Aanya, think of supply chain management as the backbone of a business. Without it, everything collapses."

She nodded, "It's like the hotel staff ensuring everything runs smoothly behind the scenes."

"Exactly," I replied, opening my door. "And just as guests would leave if the hotel didn't meet their expectations, customers would turn to competitors if businesses don't ensure product availability."

As I gathered my things, Aanya waited at the reception. She was eager to continue our conversation, and I admired her zeal. As we headed to her car, I realized that our journey of learning was far from over. The road ahead was filled with more insights and lessons to be shared.

Chapter 29: Feedback Loops: Continuous Improvement in Operations

The hum of Aanya 's car engine was soothing, and the New York streets outside bustled with activity. As we drove, her phone buzzed with a call. I listened quietly as she spoke, noting the polite but brief exchange. When she hung up, her face showed a hint of disappointment.

"That was a potential customer," she said, "but they decided not to buy."

I noticed something in her conversation. "Aanya, I couldn't help but overhear. You thanked them, which is polite, but you didn't ask for feedback. Why?"

She looked surprised. "I didn't want to be pushy. Should I have?"

I nodded, "Feedback is a gift. It's an opportunity to learn and improve."

Golden Rule: "We all need people who will give us feedback. That's how we improve." - Bill Gates

Learning: Constructive feedback is essential for growth.

1. The Importance of Feedback: Feedback helps identify areas of improvement. According to a study by Harvard Business Review, companies that prioritize feedback are 3.6 times more likely to be high-performing.

2. Constructive Criticism: It's not just about gathering feedback but understanding it. Constructive feedback can pinpoint specific areas that need attention. A Forbes study found that 92% of respondents agreed that, when given appropriately, constructive feedback is effective at improving performance.

Golden Rule: "Feedback is the breakfast of champions." - Ken Blanchard

Learning: Regular feedback nourishes growth and development.

I continued, "Think of feedback as a loop. You take an action, there's a reaction, and you use that reaction to inform your next action."

3. Implementing Feedback: Once feedback is received, it's crucial to act on it. This continuous loop ensures that operations are always improving. According to McKinsey & Company, organizations that act on feedback can see a 10-15% improvement in customer satisfaction.

4. Encouraging Feedback: It's essential to create an environment where feedback is encouraged. This can be from customers, team members, or stakeholders. A PwC survey found that 60% of employees would like feedback on a daily or weekly basis.

Golden Rule: "Your most unhappy customers are your greatest source of learning." - Bill Gates

Learning: Negative feedback, when used constructively, can lead to significant improvements.

I turned to Aanya, "Your customer's decision not to buy is valuable feedback. Maybe they found a better price, or perhaps they didn't see the value in your product. By understanding their reasons, you can refine your approach."

Aanya nodded thoughtfully, "I've always been afraid of criticism, but I see now that it's an opportunity."

We pulled up to my training venue, and I thanked her for the ride. "Remember, Aanya, feedback is a tool. Use it wisely, and it will guide you to success."

She smiled, "I will. And thank you, Dr. Vijay. Every moment with you is a lesson learned."

As I stepped out of the car, I felt a sense of accomplishment. Aanya was growing, and I was proud to be a part of her journey.

Chapter 30: The Sales Lion's Operational Mastery: Best Practices for Success

The training hall was buzzing with energy. Thousands of attendees from various industries and backgrounds had gathered, eager to learn from the best in the business. The stage was set, and the spotlight was on the mentor, a renowned figure in the sales industry.

Suddenly, the mentor's gaze fixed on me. "Dr. Vijay Viraj," he announced, "Would you please come up and share your brand's story and the best practices that have led to its success?"

The room went silent. All eyes were on me as I made my way to the stage. Taking a deep breath, I began.

1. The Power of Presentation:

"Good morning, everyone," I began, ensuring my voice was clear and confident. "Presentation isn't just about slides and visuals. It's about how you present yourself, your brand, and your story."

Golden Rule: "People don't buy what you do; they buy why you do it." - Simon Sinek, "Start With Why"

Learning: Your 'why' is the core of your brand. Present it compellingly.

I continued, "When I started my journey, I realized that the healthcare sales industry was vast. But what set the Sales Lion brand apart was our 'why'. We weren't just selling products; we were selling a vision, a promise of better healthcare."

2. Consistency is Key:

"Being consistent in your operations, your message, and your brand promise is crucial.

According to a study by Lucidpress, consistent branding across all channels increases revenue by 23%."

Golden Rule: "Success isn't always about greatness. It's about consistency. Consistent hard work leads to success. Greatness will come." - Dwayne Johnson

Learning: Consistency in operations and branding is a cornerstone of success.

3. Embrace Feedback:

I recalled our earlier conversation about feedback loops. "Feedback is a gift. It's an opportunity to refine, improve, and excel. A Harvard Business Review study found that companies that prioritize feedback are 3.6 times more likely to be high-performing."

4. The Sales Lion's Operational Best Practices:

Drawing from my personal experiences, I shared the best practices that had been instrumental in the success of the Sales Lion brand:

- Customer-Centric Approach: Always put the customer first. Understand their needs, challenges, and aspirations.
- Continuous Learning: Stay updated with the latest industry trends, technologies, and best practices.
- Collaboration: Foster a culture of collaboration within the team. A united team is a successful team.
- Innovation: Don't be afraid to try new strategies, tools, or approaches. Innovation is the key to staying ahead of the competition.

Golden Rule: "Innovation distinguishes between a leader and a follower." - Steve Jobs

Learning: Embrace innovation to lead the market.

5. The Power of Storytelling:

"Every brand has a story. It's how you tell that story that makes all the difference." I emphasized the importance of storytelling in sales, drawing parallels with everyday life situations for better understanding.

Golden Rule: "Marketing is no longer about the stuff that you make, but the stories you tell." - Seth Godin

Learning: A compelling story can resonate with customers and drive brand loyalty.

Case Study: My Journey with Unicorn Denmart Ltd.

"One of the most transformative experiences in my career was my tenure at Unicorn Denmart Ltd. as Manager of Digital Sales. The company was already a major player in the dental equipment industry, but the digital sales arena was relatively new and uncharted. My role was to establish and grow this segment."

"I faced numerous challenges – from understanding the digital landscape to training a team and establishing processes. But with a clear vision, consistent efforts, and a customer-centric approach, we achieved remarkable success. In fact, our digital sales strategies played a pivotal role in the company exceeding its sales target by 50%."

"This experience taught me the importance of adaptability, innovation, and the power of a cohesive team. It also reinforced the belief that with the right strategies and execution, any challenge can be turned into an opportunity."

As I concluded my presentation, the hall erupted in applause. The mentor nodded in approval, and I could see admiration in the eyes of the attendees.

Walking off the stage, I felt a sense of pride. Not just in my brand and its success, but in the journey, the challenges, the learnings, and the growth. The Sales Lion's operational mastery wasn't just about best practices; it was about passion, dedication, and the relentless pursuit of excellence.

Key Learnings and Golden Rules from Step 6: Operational Excellence

1. Efficiency in Processes: Streamlining sales processes can lead to increased productivity and better results.
2. Golden Rule: "Efficiency is doing things right; effectiveness is doing the right things." - Peter Drucker
3. Data-Driven Decisions: Leveraging data can provide valuable insights, leading to informed decision-making.
4. Golden Rule: "Without big data, you are blind and deaf in the middle of a freeway." - Geoffrey Moore
5. Supply Chain Significance: A robust supply chain ensures product availability; meeting customer demands promptly.
6. Golden Rule: "The more inventory a company has, the less likely they will have what they need." - Taiichi Ohno
7. Embrace Feedback: Feedback loops are essential for continuous improvement and refining operations.
8. Golden Rule: "We all need people who will give us feedback. That's how we improve." - Bill Gates
9. Operational Mastery: Consistency, innovation, and a customer-centric approach are pillars of operational success.
10. Golden Rule: "Operations keep the lights on, strategy provides a light at the end of the tunnel, but project

management is the train engine that moves the organization forward." - Joy Gumz

11. Storytelling in Sales: A compelling brand story can resonate with customers and drive brand loyalty.
12. Golden Rule: "Marketing is no longer about the stuff that you make, but the stories you tell." - Seth Godin
13. Adaptability: In the face of challenges, the ability to adapt and innovate is crucial.
14. Golden Rule: "Adaptability is about the powerful difference between adapting to cope and adapting to win." - Max McKeown
15. Collaboration: Foster a culture of collaboration for a united and successful team.
16. Golden Rule: "Alone we can do so little; together we can do so much." - Helen Keller
17. Strategic Positioning: Carve out a unique niche in the market to stand out from competitors.
18. Golden Rule: "Strategy without tactics is the slowest route to victory. Tactics without strategy is the noise before defeat." - Sun Tzu
19. Customer-Centric Approach: Always prioritize the customer's needs and challenges.
20. Golden Rule: "The purpose of a business is to create a customer." - Peter Drucker
21. Continuous Learning: Stay updated with industry trends and best practices.
22. Golden Rule: "Learning and innovation go hand in hand." - William Pollard
23. Feedback as a Gift: Use feedback as an opportunity to refine and improve.
24. Golden Rule: "Feedback is the breakfast of champions." - Ken Blanchard

25. Presentation Skills: How you present yourself and your brand can make a significant impact.
26. Golden Rule: "First impressions matter. Experts say we size up new people in somewhere between 30 seconds and two minutes." - Elliott Abrams
27. Supply Chain Efficiency: Ensuring timely product availability is key to meeting customer expectations.
28. Golden Rule: "You won't find a solution by saying there is no problem." - William Rotsler
29. Operational Consistency: Being consistent in operations and branding is a cornerstone of success.
30. Golden Rule: "Success isn't always about greatness. It's about consistency." - Dwayne Johnson

Step 7: Expanding Horizons: Global Sales and Diversification

The world of sales is vast, dynamic, and ever-evolving. As markets mature and opportunities arise, the true Sales Lion recognizes the need to venture beyond familiar territories, to explore new horizons, and to diversify. Step 7 is all about this adventurous spirit of expansion and diversification.

In today's globalized world, the boundaries that once defined markets are becoming increasingly blurred. Companies are no longer confined to their local or national markets; the entire world is a potential marketplace. But with this vast opportunity comes the challenge of understanding and adapting to diverse cultures, business practices, and consumer behaviors.

In this step, we'll embark on a journey with Dr. Vijay Viraj as he shares his experiences and insights from his global sales adventures. From understanding the nuances of entering new markets to the importance of cultural sensitivity in sales, we'll delve deep into the strategies that ensure success in global sales.

But global expansion isn't the only avenue for growth. Diversification, whether in terms of product offerings or target audiences, is another key strategy for sustainable growth. In this step, we'll explore the art and science of diversification, understanding how to identify new opportunities within and outside one's core business.

Step 7 is a testament to the limitless potential of sales. It's about thinking big, dreaming bigger, and having the courage and strategies to turn those dreams into reality. As we navigate through this step, we'll be equipped with the tools, insights, and mindset needed to expand horizons and achieve unparalleled growth in the world of sales.

Chapter 31: Entering New Markets: Strategies for Global Expansion

The sun had set, casting a warm orange hue over the city. As I stepped out of the conference venue, I noticed Aanya waiting in her car, not alone this time but accompanied by a colleague. The two seemed engrossed in a conversation, their expressions a mix of disappointment and contemplation.

Approaching the car, I tapped lightly on the window. Aanya looked up, her face lighting up with a smile, but I could sense an underlying frustration. "Dr. Vijay! Meet Sufi, my colleague. We just came from a product launch presentation. The company is trying to enter a new market with a medical device, but honestly, it felt like they missed the mark."

Sufi nodded in agreement, "Yes, it seemed like they hadn't done their homework on the new market. It's not just about launching a product; it's about understanding the nuances of the new market."

As we drove towards a renowned restaurant for dinner, Aanya curiously inquired about my day at the conference. "So, Dr. Vijay, how was your day? Any key learnings you'd like to share?"

I chuckled, "Always eager to learn, aren't you? Well, three things stood out for me today:

- The importance of cultural sensitivity when entering a new market.
- The need for thorough market research to understand local preferences.
- The significance of building local partnerships for better market penetration."

Sufi, intrigued, asked, "How do you ensure success when entering a new market?"

I thought for a moment, "Entering a new market is like setting sail into uncharted waters. You need a strong strategy, a dedicated crew, and the right tools."

Golden Rule 1: "To conquer the unknown, you must trust." - Paulo Coelho, The Alchemist. Trust in your research, your team, and most importantly, in the potential of the new market.

Golden Rule 2: "Opportunities multiply as they are seized." - Sun Tzu, The Art of War. Seizing the right opportunities at the right time can set the stage for success in a new market.

Golden Rule 3: "Change is the end result of all true learning." - Leo Buscaglia. Adapting and evolving based on market feedback is crucial.

I continued, "**Firstly**, understand the local culture and preferences. For instance, a product that's a hit in one country might not resonate with the audience in another due to cultural differences."

Aanya added, "Like how fast-food chains modify their menus based on local tastes."

"Exactly," I replied. "**Secondly**, collaborate with local partners. They have the expertise and understanding of the local market, which can be invaluable."

Sufi pondered, "But what about competition?"

I smiled, "Competition is inevitable. But if you offer something unique and valuable, and you've done your homework, you can carve out your niche."

As we reached the restaurant, the aroma of delicious food wafted through the air. Aanya quipped, "Speaking of understanding local preferences, this place surely knows its audience!"

We all laughed, realizing that whether it's food or business, understanding your audience is the key to success.

Fact: According to McKinsey & Company, companies that prioritize understanding and adapting to local cultures are 50% more likely to succeed in new markets.

Data: A Harvard Business Review study found that 58% of companies that focused on local partnerships saw a faster growth rate in new markets compared to those that didn't.

We settled into our seats at the restaurant, ready to dive into a culinary experience, I realized that the journey of entering new markets, much like a meal, is best enjoyed with preparation, understanding, and a touch of local flavor.

Chapter 32: Cultural Sensitivity in Sales: Adapting to Diverse Audiences

The ambiance of the restaurant was a blend of modern elegance and traditional charm. Soft instrumental music played in the background, creating a soothing atmosphere. As we settled into our seats, Aanya, with a twinkle in her eye, said to Sufi, "You know, Dr. Vijay has this unique way of relating food to sales methodologies. It's fascinating!"

Sufi, intrigued, looked at me and asked, "Really? How so?"

I smiled, "Well, think about it. Just as a chef tailors a dish to the palate of his audience, a salesperson must tailor their approach to the cultural and individual preferences of their clients."

Aanya added, "It's like how this restaurant has both traditional and fusion dishes. They cater to diverse tastes while staying true to the essence of the cuisine."

Sufi pondered, "So, in sales, how do you ensure you're culturally sensitive, especially when dealing with international clients?"

I replied, "It's a combination of research, empathy, and adaptability. You need to understand the cultural nuances, values, and preferences of your target audience. This not only helps in building trust but also in crafting a sales pitch that resonates with them."

Golden Rule 1: "When in Rome, do as the Romans do." - St. Ambrose. This age-old adage emphasizes the importance of adapting to the customs and behaviors of the place or group you are in.

Golden Rule 2: "Culture is more often a source of conflict than of synergy. Cultural differences are a nuisance at best and often a disaster." - Dr. Geert Hofstede, Cultures and Organizations: Software of the Mind. Recognizing and respecting cultural differences is crucial in sales.

Golden Rule 3: "The strength of the team is each individual member. The strength of each member is the team." - Phil Jackson, Eleven Rings: The Soul of Success. Emphasizing the importance of a diverse team that brings varied cultural insights to the table.

Aanya asked, "But isn't it challenging to keep up with so many cultural nuances?"

I responded, "It is, but that's where a diverse sales team comes into play. Having team members from different cultural backgrounds can provide invaluable insights. They can guide the team on cultural dos and don'ts."

Sufi, looking thoughtful, said, "So, it's not just about selling a product or service, but about selling an experience that aligns with the client's cultural values."

"Exactly," I replied. "And the more culturally sensitive and adaptable you are, the more successful you'll be in building lasting relationships with clients from diverse backgrounds."

Fact: According to a study by the Harvard Business Review, companies that prioritize cultural sensitivity in their sales strategies see a 35% increase in client retention.

Data: A survey by Forbes found that 72% of respondents were more likely to purchase a product or service if the sales approach was culturally tailored to them.

As our conversation flowed, the waiter arrived with a platter of assorted delicacies. Aanya remarked, "Look at the presentation! It's a blend of the traditional and the modern. Just like a culturally sensitive sales approach."

We all nodded in agreement, realizing that whether in food or sales, understanding and respecting cultural nuances makes all the difference.

Chapter 33: The Sales Lion's Global Adventures: Lessons from International Sales

The restaurant's atmosphere was light and jovial. Between bites of delicious food, we shared stories, jokes, and insights. At one point, I turned to Sufi and asked, "So, Sufi, if you were to sell a product to someone from a completely different culture, how would you approach it?"

Sufi thought for a moment and replied, "I'd probably start by researching their culture, understanding their needs, and then tailoring my pitch accordingly."

I chuckled, "That's a good start! But let me share a joke with you. Why did the salesperson bring a map to the sales meeting? To 'navigate' the deal!" We all laughed, and the mood lightened further.

Aanya, always curious, then asked, "Have you ever faced challenges in international sales? I mean, selling to clients from different countries and cultures?"

I nodded, "Absolutely. Let me share a story from my time selling dental equipment in Japan. The Japanese market is very different from the Indian market. They value precision, punctuality, and presentation. During one of my presentations, I made the mistake of being a tad bit casual, thinking my product's features would speak for themselves. But the clients weren't impressed. I quickly realized that in Japan, the way you present is as important as what you present."

Golden Rule 1: "To effectively communicate, we must realize that we are all different in the way we perceive the world and use this understanding as a guide to our communication with others." - Tony Robbins, Unlimited Power. Emphasizing the importance of understanding cultural perceptions.

Golden Rule 2: "Don't find customers for your products, find products for your customers." - Seth Godin, This Is Marketing. Highlighting the need to tailor products and pitches to the specific needs of the audience.

Golden Rule 3: "Your culture is your brand." - Tony Hsieh, Delivering Happiness. A reminder that understanding and integrating into a culture can significantly enhance brand perception.

Fact: According to McKinsey & Company, companies that understand and adapt to local cultures are 60% more likely to succeed in international markets.

Data: A survey by the International Sales Institute found that 80% of international sales failures were due to cultural misunderstandings.

I continued, "After that experience in Japan, I took it upon myself to immerse myself in the culture. I learned basic Japanese, understood their business etiquette, and even adopted some of their presentation styles. The next time I pitched, it was a resounding success."

Sufi, intrigued, asked, "So, it's all about adapting and understanding the client's perspective?"

I nodded, "Exactly. And speaking of understanding perspectives," I said, turning to Sufi with a playful glint in my eye, "Imagine you're my international client. How would I convince you to invest in my mentorship program?"

Sufi smirked, "Try me."

Over the next few minutes, I pitched my mentorship program, highlighting its unique features, tailoring it to Sufi's needs, and emphasizing the value it would bring to her. By the end of it, Sufi was thoroughly impressed.

She exclaimed, "That was brilliant! You've got yourself a deal." And with a flourish, she handed me a cheque for 5000 US dollars.

Aanya clapped, "That was a live demo right there!"

I smiled, "Sales, my dear Aanya, is not just about selling a product. It's about selling an experience, a journey, and most importantly, a relationship."

As we wrapped up our dinner, we all left with a deeper understanding of the intricacies of sales, especially in the international arena. The night was a testament to the power of stories, experiences, and the art of selling.

Chapter 34: Diversifying Product Offerings: Expanding Your Portfolio

The car ride back to the hotel was filled with the soft hum of the engine and the occasional honk from the bustling New York streets. Aanya, ever the inquisitive one, turned to me and asked, "You've talked a lot about selling and understanding the market. But how do you decide what products to sell in the first place?"

I smiled, "That's a great question, Aanya. It's all about diversifying your product offerings. Just like in investments, you don't put all your eggs in one basket. In sales, especially in a dynamic field like healthcare, you need to have a diverse portfolio."

Sufi chimed in, "But how do you decide which products to add to your portfolio?"

Golden Rule 1: "Diversification is a protection against ignorance. It makes very little sense for those who know what they're doing." - Warren Buffett. This emphasizes the importance of understanding the market and the products you're diversifying into.

Fact: According to the Harvard Business Review, companies that diversified their product offerings were 30% more likely to outperform their non-diversified competitors in terms of revenue.

I explained, "It's a mix of market research, understanding customer needs, and sometimes, a bit of intuition. For instance, at Unicorn Denmart, we realized that while we had a strong portfolio of dental equipment, there was a growing demand for more advanced, tech-driven solutions. So, we expanded our portfolio to include digital imaging systems, which turned out to be a game-changer."

Aanya pondered, "So, it's about keeping an ear to the ground and being ready to adapt?"

"Exactly," I replied. "And sometimes, it's also about creating a need. Introducing a product so revolutionary that the market doesn't know they need it until they see it."

Golden Rule 2: "Innovation distinguishes between a leader and a follower." - Steve Jobs, Apple. Highlighting the importance of being at the forefront of product innovation.

Data: A study by the Sales Innovation Institute found that 70% of top-performing companies regularly updated and diversified their product offerings, compared to just 40% of average-performing companies.

Sufi, looking thoughtful, said, "So, diversifying isn't just about adding more products, but about adding the right products."

I nodded, "Precisely. And it's also about knowing when to phase out products that are no longer relevant."

Golden Rule 3: "It's not about ideas. It's about making ideas happen." - Scott Belsky, Behance. Emphasizing the importance of execution in product diversification.

As we neared the hotel, I concluded, "Diversifying product offerings is like crafting a well-balanced meal. Each product should complement the other, fulfilling different needs, but together, they should form a cohesive, comprehensive portfolio."

Aanya smiled, "Speaking of meals, tonight's dinner and conversation were food for thought. Thank you for the insights."

I chuckled, "Always happy to share, Aanya. And remember, in sales and in life, diversity is the spice that makes everything nice."

With that, we reached the hotel, our minds enriched and our spirits high, eager for the next day's learnings and adventures.

Key Learnings and Golden Rules from Step 7: Expanding Horizons

1. Understanding Local Nuances: When entering new markets, it's crucial to understand the local culture, customs, and consumer behavior. Tailoring your approach to fit the local context can significantly enhance success rates.
2. Golden Rule: "When in Rome, do as the Romans do." Emphasize the importance of adapting to local cultures when expanding globally.
3. Cultural Sensitivity: Being aware of and respecting cultural differences can pave the way for smoother interactions and negotiations in international sales.
4. Golden Rule: "Diversity is a fact, inclusion is a choice." - Justin Trudeau. This highlights the importance of inclusive practices in global sales.
5. Learning from Failures: Every market will pose its unique challenges. Learning from failures and adapting strategies accordingly is key to long-term success.
6. Golden Rule: "Innovation distinguishes between a leader and a follower." - Steve Jobs. Emphasizing the importance of being at the forefront of product innovation, especially in diverse markets.
7. The Power of Local Partnerships: Collaborating with local partners can provide invaluable insights and facilitate smoother market entry.
8. Golden Rule: "Alone we can do so little; together we can do so much." - Helen Keller. Stressing the importance of collaboration in global expansion.
9. Diversification as a Growth Strategy: Expanding product offerings based on market needs can lead to increased revenue streams and reduced business risks.

10. Golden Rule: "Diversification is a protection against ignorance. It makes very little sense for those who know what they're doing." - Warren Buffett. This emphasizes the importance of understanding the market and the products you're diversifying into.
11. Personal Touch in Sales: Even in global sales, personal interactions, understanding client needs, and building genuine relationships can set you apart from competitors.
12. Golden Rule: "People do business with people, not companies." Highlighting the importance of personal relationships in sales.
13. Continuous Learning: The global market is ever-evolving. Staying updated with global trends, market shifts, and consumer behavior is essential.
14. Golden Rule: "It's not about ideas. It's about making ideas happen." - Scott Belsky. Emphasizing the importance of execution in product diversification.
15. Feedback is Gold: Especially when diversifying or entering new markets, feedback from local teams, partners, and customers can provide invaluable insights for improvement and growth.

With these learnings and golden rules, sales professionals can navigate the complex waters of global sales and diversification, ensuring success across borders and cultures.

Step 8: The Art of Negotiation

Every salesperson, at some point in their career, finds themselves at the crossroads of a high-stakes negotiation. It's an arena where the balance of power, strategy, and interpersonal skills come into play, determining the outcome of a deal. Step 8 delves deep into this intricate dance of negotiation, revealing the nuances, tactics, and strategies that can make or break a deal.

Negotiation is more than just a transactional exchange; it's an art form. It requires a deep understanding of human psychology, a keen sense of timing, and the ability to read between the lines. It's about finding common ground, building rapport, and crafting win-win solutions that benefit all parties involved.

In this step, we'll journey alongside Dr. Vijay Viraj as he shares his wealth of experiences from the negotiation table. From preparing for high-stakes discussions to understanding the dynamics of power and influence, we'll uncover the secrets behind successful negotiations.

We'll also delve into the importance of empathy in negotiation, understanding the perspectives and motivations of the other side. Through real-life case studies and reflections, we'll learn how to navigate challenges, handle resistance, and seal deals that foster long-term relationships and mutual success.

Step 8 is a masterclass in the art of negotiation. It's about equipping oneself with the skills, strategies, and mindset to navigate the complex world of deal-making, ensuring that every negotiation leads to fruitful outcomes and strengthened relationships.

Chapter 35: Setting the Stage: Preparing for High-Stakes Discussions

The sun had barely risen, casting a soft golden hue over the city. As I walked into the hotel's breakfast area, I noticed Aanya already seated at a corner table, engrossed in some notes. Her dedication was evident, but as I approached her, I noticed a slight pallor on her face.

"Good morning, Aanya," I greeted, extending my hand.

She looked up, her eyes brightening with a smile, "Good morning, Dr. Vijay." As our hands met in a firm handshake, I could feel the warmth of her hand, indicating a mild fever.

"You're running a fever," I remarked with concern.

She chuckled lightly, "You've got quite the observant eye. But don't worry, it's just a slight fever. Nothing that can keep me from our learning sessions."

I raised an eyebrow, impressed, "Your ability to negotiate your way into continuing our discussion despite not feeling well is commendable. It reminds me of the importance of preparation in high-stakes discussions."

Aanya leaned in, eager to absorb every word. "Tell me more," she urged.

1. Research is Your Best Friend

Before any negotiation, it's crucial to gather as much information as possible. Understand the market conditions, the needs of the other party, and the potential challenges that might arise. This knowledge will not only give you confidence but will also allow you to anticipate the moves of the other party.

Golden Rule: "The only source of knowledge is experience." - Albert Einstein. This emphasizes the importance of learning from past negotiations and using that knowledge in future discussions.

2. Understand Your BATNA (Best Alternative To a Negotiated Agreement)

Always have a clear understanding of what your alternatives are if the negotiation doesn't go as planned. This not only gives you a safety net but also strengthens your position during the discussion.

3. Set Clear Objectives

Before entering any negotiation, be clear about what you want to achieve. This clarity will guide your strategy and help you stay focused on the end goal.

Golden Rule: "The man who does not know where he wants to go, cannot grow." - Napoleon Hill. This rule emphasizes the importance of having clear goals in any endeavor, including negotiations.

4. Role Play

Practice makes perfect. Before a significant negotiation, role-playing can help you anticipate potential questions, objections, and counteroffers. It also helps in refining your pitch and understanding potential weaknesses in your argument.

5. Create a Positive Environment

The ambiance and setting of a negotiation can significantly influence its outcome. Ensure that the environment is conducive to open dialogue and mutual respect.

Golden Rule: "The environment is where we all meet; where we all have a mutual interest; it is the one thing all of us share." - Lady Bird Johnson. This rule, though originally about nature, can be applied to the importance of creating a positive environment for negotiations.

6. Be Ready to Walk Away

Sometimes, the best decision is to walk away from a negotiation if it doesn't align with your objectives or values. This doesn't signify defeat but shows strength in prioritizing long-term benefits over short-term gains.

As I finished, I took a sip of my coffee and looked at Aanya. "Remember, negotiation isn't just about winning. It's about finding a solution that benefits both parties."

Aanya nodded, processing the information. "So, preparation is more than just knowing facts. It's about understanding the dynamics, setting the right environment, and being mentally prepared for any outcome."

"Exactly," I replied. "And speaking of dynamics, do you know how to maintain your ground without seeming too aggressive or too passive?"

She looked intrigued, "Tell me more." I smiled, "Well, that's a story for our next discussion."

Chapter 36: The Sales Lion's Negotiation Tactics: Winning Deals without Losing Ground

After getting ready for my conference, I came back to Aanya waiting for me at the reception.

"Dr. Vijay," she began, her voice filled with anticipation, "you left me with quite the thought-provoking question earlier. How do you strike that balance in negotiations?"

I smiled, appreciating her eagerness. "Ah, diving right in, are we? Very well. Negotiation is an art, and like any art, it requires practice, understanding, and a few tricks up your sleeve."

As we walked towards Aanya 's car, I began to delve into the intricacies of negotiation.

"First and foremost, it's essential to understand that negotiation isn't about winning or losing. It's about finding a middle ground where both parties feel they've achieved something valuable."

Aanya nodded, taking mental notes. "So, what are some of your go-to tactics?"

Golden Rule #1 (from "Getting to Yes" by Roger Fisher and William Ury): "Separate the people from the problem." It's crucial to address the issue at hand and not let personal feelings or biases cloud the negotiation process.

"In my early days at Unicorn Denmart, I had to negotiate with suppliers who had been in the business for decades. It was intimidating, but by focusing on the problem and not letting personal dynamics interfere, I was able to secure deals that were beneficial for both parties."

Golden Rule #2 (from "Influence: The Psychology of Persuasion" by Robert B. Cialdini): "Leverage the principle of reciprocity." When you offer something of value, the other party is more inclined to reciprocate with a concession of their own.

"I remember a time when we were introducing a new dental product in the market. By offering training sessions to our clients, we not only showcased the product's value but also built trust. This led to more substantial and more extended contracts."

Golden Rule #3 (from "Never Split the Difference" by Chris Voss): "Use tactical empathy." Understand the emotions and motivations of the other party. By validating their feelings and perspective, you can navigate the conversation towards a mutually beneficial outcome.

"During a particularly challenging negotiation with a competitor, I realized they were hesitant because of market uncertainties. By acknowledging their concerns and offering a phased approach to our deal, we were able to move forward."

Aanya seemed deep in thought as we reached her car. "These tactics... they're not just about business, are they? They're about understanding people."

I nodded, "Exactly. At its core, negotiation is about human interaction. And the better you understand people, the more successful you'll be in finding common ground."

As she unlocked her car, Aanya turned to me, her eyes reflecting a mix of gratitude and determination. "Thank you, Dr. Vijay. Every conversation with you is a masterclass in itself."

I chuckled, "Just remember, negotiation is a journey, not a destination. Keep learning, keep adapting."

Chapter 37: Understanding the Other Side: Empathy in Negotiation

The hum of the car's engine was the only sound for a few moments as we pulled away from the hotel. Aanya seemed focused on the road, but I could sense a whirlwind of thoughts behind her eyes.

Breaking the silence, I asked, "Aanya, have you ever felt truly understood by someone?"

She glanced at me, a hint of surprise in her eyes. "That's an unexpected question, Dr. Vijay. But to answer you, not often. Why do you ask?"

I leaned back, choosing my words carefully. "Empathy, Aanya, is the cornerstone of effective negotiation. It's about truly understanding the other side, not just their words but their emotions, motivations, and fears."

Golden Rule #1 (from "Emotional Intelligence" by Daniel Goleman): "Empathy doesn't mean agreeing with the other person but understanding their perspective." It's the ability to step into someone else's shoes, see the world through their eyes, and feel what they feel.

Aanya pondered this. "So, it's not just about understanding the business side of things but the human side as well?"

"Exactly," I replied. "In sales, and in life, people want to feel heard and understood. When you show genuine empathy, you build trust, which is invaluable in any negotiation."

Golden Rule #2 (from "Difficult Conversations" by Douglas Stone, Bruce Patton, and Sheila Heen): "Every conversation has three dimensions: the 'What happened?' conversation, the 'Feelings' conversation, and the 'Identity' conversation." Recognizing and addressing these layers can lead to more profound, more meaningful interactions.

I continued, "Aanya, think about a time when you felt misunderstood. How did that make you feel?"

She hesitated, then shared, "It was during a family gathering. I tried to explain my career choices to my relatives, but they just couldn't understand. It felt isolating, like I was speaking a different language."

I nodded, "That's a common feeling. Now, imagine a client or a competitor feeling the same way. If you can bridge that gap of misunderstanding, you've already won half the battle."

Golden Rule #3 (from "How to Win Friends and Influence People" by Dale Carnegie): "Seek first to understand, then to be understood." By prioritizing understanding, you pave the way for more effective communication and negotiation.

As we neared the conference venue, Aanya's expression turned introspective. "Dr. Vijay, I've been so focused on pushing my agenda that I've forgotten to truly listen. In my personal life too, I've made decisions without considering others' feelings."

A tear glistened in her eye as she parked the car. "Thank you for this lesson. It's more valuable than any sales technique."

I smiled gently, placing a reassuring hand on her shoulder. "Remember, Aanya, empathy is a skill. It can be cultivated and refined. And it will serve you well, both in sales and in life."

As I stepped out of the car, I turned to her, "I'll see you this evening for dinner?"

She nodded, wiping away a tear, "Yes, Dr. Vijay. I look forward to it."

Chapter 38: Sealing the Deal: Closing Techniques for Success

The evening sun cast a warm glow as I stepped out of the conference venue. To my pleasant surprise, Aanya was waiting for me, looking radiant in a tasteful ensemble. "You look wonderful, Aanya," I complimented as we settled into the backseat of her car.

She smiled, "Thank you, Dr. Vijay. I thought I'd dress up a bit for our dinner. But first, I have so many questions from our conversation this morning."

I chuckled, "I had a feeling you would. Go on."

began, "In sales, how do you know when it's the right time to close a deal? And how do you ensure the client is truly convinced?"

I pondered for a moment. "Closing a deal is an art, Aanya. It's about recognizing signals, understanding needs, and offering value."

Golden Rule #1 (from "The Psychology of Selling" by Brian Tracy): "Always be closing." This doesn't mean being pushy but rather continuously looking for opportunities to provide value and move the sale forward.

She nodded, jotting down notes. "But what if a client is hesitant or has reservations?"

"That's where your closing techniques come into play," I explained. "For instance, there's the 'Now or Never Close,' where you make the offer so enticing that the client feels they'd miss out if they didn't act immediately."

Golden Rule #2 (from "SPIN Selling" by Neil Rackham): "Address objections before they arise." By understanding potential concerns and addressing them proactively, you position yourself as a trusted advisor.

Aanya looked intrigued. "Can you share a real-life example?"

I smiled, recalling a memorable experience. "Certainly. While I was at Unicorn Denmart, I had a challenging client, a dentist who had already booked a machine from a competitor. But I believed in the value of our premium CBCT machine. Over several meetings, I showcased its unique features, offered training sessions, and even introduced him to other satisfied clients. I continuously added value, ensuring he recognized the long-term benefits of our product."

She leaned in, engrossed. "And then?"

"After weeks of persistence and demonstrating genuine care for his practice's success, he canceled his order with the competitor and chose our machine."

Aanya 's eyes widened. "That's incredible! So, it's all about persistence and value addition?"

I nodded. "Exactly. And also timing. Recognizing when a client is ready to make a decision and then presenting them with a compelling reason to choose you."

Golden Rule #3 (from "Influence: The Psychology of Persuasion" by Robert B. Cialdini): "People want what they can't have." Creating a sense of scarcity or exclusivity can often tip the scales in your favor.

As the car pulled up to the restaurant, Aanya looked thoughtful. "Dr. Vijay, every conversation with you feels like a masterclass. I can't wait to apply these techniques."

I smiled, "And I'm sure you'll master them in no time. Now, shall we enjoy our dinner?"

Chapter 39: Post-Negotiation Reflections: Learning and Growing from Every Interaction

The restaurant's ambiance was serene, with soft lighting and a gentle hum of conversations around us. As we settled into our seats, I noticed Aanya deep in thought.

Breaking the silence, I asked, "Aanya, do you remember your first job interview?"

She looked up, surprised. "Yes, I do. Why?"

"I'm curious," I began, "How did you negotiate your salary or position during your review cycles?"

Aanya chuckled, "Ah, that. Well, during my first job interview, I was so eager to get the job that I accepted the first offer they gave me. But over time, as I proved my worth and took on more responsibilities, I learned the art of negotiation. By my third review cycle, I had successfully negotiated a significant raise and a better position."

I nodded appreciatively. "That's impressive. Negotiation isn't just about the immediate deal; it's about setting the stage for future interactions and growth."

She looked intrigued. "How so?"

"Well, every negotiation, whether successful or not, offers a learning opportunity. Reflecting on these interactions helps us understand our strengths, areas of improvement, and how to better approach future negotiations."

Golden Rule #1 (from "Never Split the Difference" by Chris Voss): "Negotiation is not an act of battle; it's a process of discovery." The goal is to uncover as much information as possible.

Aanya sipped her drink, then asked, "What about you? How did you negotiate your way up the corporate ladder?"

I smiled, recalling my journey. "In my early career, I started at a junior level. But with dedication, hard work, and continuous learning, I climbed the ranks. Within five years, I grew my salary by six times and went through five designations, eventually becoming the Divisional Country Sales Head, Vice President. It wasn't just about negotiating salary but also roles, responsibilities, and opportunities."

Golden Rule #2 (from "Getting to Yes" by Roger Fisher and William Ury): "Separate the people from the problem." Focus on the issue at hand and not on personalities or emotions.

She looked impressed. "That's quite an achievement. But how did you ensure that you continued to grow and learn from every interaction?"

I leaned forward, "By always reflecting post-negotiation. Whether I sealed a deal or faced rejection, I analyzed the interaction. What went well? What could I have done differently? This reflection helped me refine my approach, making me a better negotiator with each interaction."

Golden Rule #3 (from "The Art of Negotiation" by Michael Wheeler): "The road to success is paved with mistakes well-handled." It's not about avoiding mistakes but learning from them.

Aanya nodded, taking notes. "So, it's a continuous cycle of negotiation, reflection, learning, and growth?"

"Exactly," I affirmed. "And with each cycle, you not only become a better negotiator but also a better version of yourself."

As we delved into our meal, the conversation shifted to lighter topics. But the essence of our discussion lingered, emphasizing the importance of continuous learning and growth in every aspect of life.

Chapter 40: Types of Negotiation Skills and Strategies

The night had deepened, and the city lights shimmered outside. As Aanya 's car glided through the streets, the silence inside was palpable. I leaned back, reflecting on our conversations, when Aanya 's voice broke the stillness.

"You know, there's something I've always been curious about," she began, her voice hesitant yet determined. "The different types of negotiation skills and strategies. I've read about them, but I've never had someone explain them to me in depth."

I smiled, "Aanya, that's premium knowledge. It's not something I usually share openly."

She glanced at me, a playful glint in her eyes. "Come on, after all our discussions, you owe me this one."

I chuckled, "Trying to negotiate with a negotiator, are we?"

She grinned, "Maybe. Or maybe I'm just trying to learn from the best."

I sighed, "Alright, alright. But remember, these are powerful tools. Use them wisely."

Aanya nodded eagerly, and I began.

1. Distributive Negotiation: This is a win-lose situation where one party's gain is another party's loss. It's like dividing a pie; the bigger piece one person gets, the smaller the other person's piece.

Golden Rule (from "Bargaining for Advantage" by G. Richard Shell): "Know your BATNA (Best Alternative To a Negotiated Agreement). It gives you the power to walk away."

2. Integrative Negotiation: Here, both parties look for a win-win solution. It's about expanding the pie rather than dividing it.

Golden Rule (from "Getting More" by Stuart Diamond): "Find and leverage common interests. It's the key to creating value."

3. Competitive Negotiation: This is where you push for what you want, often at the expense of the other party.

Golden Rule (from "The Art of Woo" by G. Richard Shell & Mario Moussa): "Build relationships, not just transactions. Long-term success is built on trust."

4. Collaborative Negotiation: Both parties work together to achieve the best outcome for all involved.

Golden Rule (from "Negotiation Genius" by Deepak Malhotra & Max Bazerman): "Seek first to understand, then to be understood."

5. Avoidance: Sometimes, the best strategy is to avoid negotiation until you're better prepared or the circumstances are more favorable.

Golden Rule (from "Difficult Conversations" by Douglas Stone, Bruce Patton, & Sheila Heen): "Timing is everything. Choose your moments wisely."

6. Accommodation: This is where one party gives in to the other. It's not about being weak but about choosing battles.

Golden Rule (from "Influence: The Psychology of Persuasion" by Robert B. Cialdini): "Reciprocity is powerful. Sometimes, giving in can lead to bigger gains in the future."

I paused, taking a breath. "These are just the basics, Aanya. Each strategy has its time and place, and the key is to know when to use which one."

Aanya looked deep in thought. "Thank you," she whispered, her voice filled with gratitude. "This... this is invaluable."

As we pulled up to the hotel, she turned to me, her eyes shining. "I can't thank you enough for everything you've shared."

I smiled, "It was my pleasure. Remember, knowledge is power, but only when applied wisely."

She nodded, then, in a spontaneous gesture, leaned over and gave me a hug. "Thank you," she murmured again.

As I stepped out of the car, I couldn't help but think about the impact of sharing knowledge. It wasn't just about imparting information; it was about empowering others to be their best selves.

Key Learnings and Golden Rules from Step 8: The Art of Negotiation

1. Preparation is Key: Before entering any negotiation, ensure you're well-prepared with all the necessary information and a clear understanding of your objectives.
2. Know Your Worth: Always be aware of your value proposition and how it stands out from the competition.
3. Golden Rule (from "Bargaining for Power" by Jeffrey Krivis): "Negotiation is not about winning or losing; it's about achieving a mutually beneficial outcome."
4. Active Listening: Paying close attention to what the other party is saying can provide valuable insights and help in formulating a more effective negotiation strategy.
5. Golden Rule (from "Influence: The Psychology of Persuasion" by Robert B. Cialdini): "People are more likely to say 'yes' to those they like."
6. Empathy is Powerful: Understanding and acknowledging the emotions and motivations of the other party can lead to more fruitful negotiations.
7. Golden Rule (from "Getting More" by Stuart Diamond): "Find and leverage common interests. It's the key to creating value."
8. Closing is an Art: Mastering the techniques to seal the deal is crucial. This includes understanding when to push, when to hold back, and when to compromise.

9. Golden Rule (from "The Art of Closing the Sale" by Brian Tracy): "Always be solution-oriented. Focus on how you can solve the other party's problems."
10. Reflect and Learn: After every negotiation, take the time to reflect on what went well, what could've been done better, and how you can improve in the future.
11. Golden Rule (from "Never Split the Difference" by Chris Voss): "Every negotiation is an opportunity to learn more about yourself and the other party."
12. Diversify Your Negotiation Tactics: Different situations call for different strategies. Be flexible and adaptable.
13. Golden Rule (from "Negotiation Genius" by Deepak Malhotra & Max Bazerman): "Seek first to understand, then to be understood."
14. Avoidance Can Be Strategic: Sometimes, the best negotiation move is to wait for a more opportune moment.
15. Build Long-Term Relationships: Negotiation isn't just about the immediate deal; it's about building a relationship that can lead to more opportunities in the future.
16. Golden Rule (from "Difficult Conversations" by Douglas Stone, Bruce Patton, & Sheila Heen): "Timing is everything. Choose your moments wisely."
17. Understand Different Negotiation Types: From distributive to integrative, each type has its own set of strategies and tactics.
18. Golden Rule (from "Bargaining for Advantage" by G. Richard Shell): "Know your BATNA (Best Alternative To a Negotiated Agreement). It gives you the power to walk away."

19. Continuous Improvement: Always seek to refine and improve your negotiation skills. The world of sales is ever-evolving, and so should your tactics.
20. Golden Rule (from "The Secrets of Power Negotiating" by Roger Dawson): "In negotiation, the one who cares less, wins. Be willing to walk away, but do so with respect."

Step 9: Adapting to Market Changes

The only constant in the world of sales, especially in the dynamic healthcare sector, is change. Markets evolve, technologies disrupt, and customer preferences shift. In such a volatile environment, the ability to adapt, innovate, and stay ahead of the curve becomes the defining trait of a successful sales professional. Step 9 is dedicated to this very essence of adaptability and the strategies required to thrive amidst market changes.

In this pivotal step, we'll explore the ever-changing landscape of healthcare sales. We'll delve into the challenges and opportunities that arise from market shifts and how to position oneself advantageously amidst these changes. Through Dr. Vijay Viraj's experiences and insights, we'll learn the importance of continuous learning, staying updated with industry trends, and the art of predicting market movements.

Furthermore, we'll discuss the significance of innovation in sales. How can one embrace new techniques, tools, and technologies to stay relevant? How does one pivot their sales approach when faced with unforeseen challenges or new market realities?

Through real-world examples, case studies, and Dr. Viraj's invaluable insights, we'll uncover strategies for reinventing one's sales approach, ensuring resilience and relevance in a constantly evolving market. This step is a testament to the fact that adaptability isn't just a skill; it's a mindset, a philosophy that ensures sustained success in the world of sales.

Chapter 41: The Ever-Changing Healthcare Landscape: Staying Updated

The sun had barely risen over the iconic New York skyline when Aanya, with a mix of excitement and anticipation, entered the hotel's breakfast area. She had hoped to catch Dr. Vijay early, to maximize their learning time together. However, the receptionist informed her that he had left early for a meditation session at his conference and would return later. A bit disappointed but understanding the importance of mindfulness, especially in a bustling city like New York, Aanya decided to wait.

The next morning, she was back, punctual as ever. As she sipped her coffee, she noticed Dr. Vijay entering the restaurant. His calm demeanor was evident, probably an aftereffect of his meditation. They exchanged warm greetings, and Aanya couldn't help but express her admiration for his dedication to mindfulness amidst his busy schedule.

Dr. Vijay smiled, "Just like the healthcare landscape, our minds are ever-evolving. Staying updated and centered is crucial."

Aanya, always eager to learn, probed, "Speaking of the healthcare landscape, how do you keep up with its rapid changes?"

Dr. Vijay took a moment and then began, "The healthcare industry, much like this city, is always on the move. New technologies, regulations, patient needs... it's a whirlwind. But there are ways to stay ahead."

Golden Rule 1: "Always be a student. Continuous learning is the key." (Reference: "The Fifth Discipline" by Peter Senge)

He continued, "Did you know that in the last decade, telemedicine consultations have grown by over 400%? Or that AI-driven diagnostic tools are predicted to reduce hospital costs by around 50% by 2030?"

Aanya 's eyes widened. "That's impressive! But how does one adapt to such rapid shifts?"

Golden Rule 2: "Embrace change, don't resist it. The more adaptable you are, the more opportunities you'll find." (Reference: "Who Moved My Cheese?" by Dr. Spencer Johnson)

Dr. Vijay elaborated, "When I was with Unicorn Denmart, we constantly had to adapt to new dental technologies. It was a challenge, but also an opportunity. By staying updated, we could offer the latest solutions to our clients, giving us an edge."

Aanya thoughtfully remarked, "It's like this city. Always changing, always evolving. But those who adapt thrive."

"Exactly," Dr. Vijay responded. "And it's not just about adapting but anticipating. By predicting where the industry is headed, you can position yourself advantageously."

Golden Rule 3: "Network extensively. Your peers, competitors, and even clients can offer invaluable insights into upcoming trends." (Reference: "Never Eat Alone" by Keith Ferrazzi)

As they enjoyed their breakfast, the conversation flowed seamlessly from personal experiences to industry insights. Aanya felt enriched, not just by the knowledge but by the way Dr. Vijay related it to real-world scenarios.

As they wrapped up, Dr. Vijay left Aanya with a thought, "Remember, in the world of sales, and especially in healthcare, knowledge isn't just power; it's survival."

Aanya nodded, already looking forward to their next discussion.

Chapter 42: Innovation in Sales: Embracing New Techniques and Technologies

At the breakfast table, Aanya was still processing the insights from our earlier discussion, occasionally jotting down notes in her journal.

"I've been thinking about what you said earlier," she began, "about the ever-changing healthcare landscape. It's fascinating how quickly things evolve."

I nodded, taking a sip of my coffee. "Absolutely. And it's not just healthcare. Every industry is in a state of flux, and sales professionals need to be at the forefront of these changes."

Just then, my phone buzzed with a notification. Glancing at it, I smiled. "Looks like my conference has wrapped up earlier than expected. I have the next three days free to explore New York."

Aanya 's eyes lit up. "That's fantastic! How about I show you around? There's a tech pop-up event in Times Square today. Startups are showcasing their latest innovations. I think you'll find it interesting."

Intrigued, I agreed. As we made our way to Times Square, the event was in full swing. Startups from various sectors were displaying their cutting-edge technologies. Aanya was particularly captivated by a booth that showcased an AI-driven diagnostic tool for healthcare.

"This could be a game-changer," she remarked.

I nodded in agreement. "Innovation is crucial in sales. Embracing new techniques and technologies can give you a significant competitive advantage."

Golden Rule 1: "Stay curious. The world of sales is ever-evolving. The best salespeople are those who constantly seek out new knowledge and techniques." (Reference: "The Innovator's Dilemma" by Clayton M. Christensen)

As we wandered through the event, I shared anecdotes from my past, including how, during my tenure at Unicorn Denmart, we had integrated a groundbreaking dental imaging technology that had significantly boosted our sales.

Aanya looked thoughtful. "But how do you determine which innovations to embrace?"

Golden Rule 2: "Always prioritize the customer. If an innovation enhances the customer experience or meets a previously unaddressed need, it's worth considering." (Reference: "Outside In" by Harley Manning and Kerry Bodine)

I pointed to a startup showcasing a virtual reality tool for medical training. "See that? It might seem like a novelty now, but in a few years, it could be a standard training tool. Being able to anticipate and adapt to such shifts is crucial."

Golden Rule 3: "Innovation isn't just about technology. It's also about approaches, strategies, and mindsets. Stay open to change, and don't be afraid to take calculated risks." (Reference: "Innovator's DNA" by Jeff Dyer, Hal Gregersen, and Clayton M. Christensen)

As we left the event and moved towards food court, the vibrant energy of New York surrounded us, a testament to the city's innovative spirit. Aanya turned to me, gratitude evident in her eyes. "Thank you for the wisdom. Every moment with you is a lesson."

Chapter 43: The Sales Lion's Adaptability: Thriving in a Dynamic Environment

The bustling energy of Times Square was palpable, even more so in the startup event. After our enlightening walk through the tech pop-ups, Aanya and I decided to grab a bite at one of the food stalls. The aroma of sizzling street food wafted through the air, and we settled down with our plates, the city's iconic skyline serving as our backdrop.

Aanya, ever the curious learner, took a moment before diving into her questions. "You've spoken a lot about innovation and staying updated, but how do you personally adapt to changes, especially unexpected ones?"

I took a bite, pondering her question. "Adaptability is a mindset. It's about being open to change and not being too rigid in your ways."

Aanya: "Can you recall a time when you had to drastically change your approach because of unforeseen market changes?"

I nodded, "Absolutely. During my tenure at Unicorn Denmart, there was a sudden shift in dental equipment preferences. Instead of resisting the change, I quickly adapted our sales strategies, focusing on customer feedback and market trends. This allowed us to stay ahead of the curve."

Aanya: "How do you ensure that your team is also adaptable?"

"Continuous training and fostering a culture of learning. Encouraging them to be curious, to question, and to not fear failure."

Aanya: "What's the biggest challenge you've faced in adapting to a new environment?"

"Understanding the nuances of different cultures when expanding globally. But with research, patience, and a willingness to learn, I overcame those challenges."

Aanya: "How do you stay motivated when faced with constant change?"

"By focusing on the bigger picture. Change is inevitable, but if you have a clear vision and purpose, you can navigate through any storm."

Aanya: "Do you believe adaptability can be taught?"

"Yes, but it also requires a willingness to change. It's a combination of mindset and action."

As our conversation flowed, the sun began to set, casting a golden hue over Times Square. Aany , with a mischievous glint in her eye, said, "How about we explore the nightlife of New York? There's a club I know that perfectly captures the city's dynamic spirit."

I raised an eyebrow, intrigued. "Nightlife? What's so special about it?"

Aanya grinned, "New York's nightlife is legendary. It's where cultures blend, music transcends, and every moment is a celebration of life. Plus, it's the perfect place to observe adaptability in action – from the DJ reading the room and changing tracks to the mixologist crafting drinks based on individual preferences."

Chuckling at her persuasive pitch, I agreed, "Alright, let's experience this legendary nightlife."

And with that, we set off, ready to embrace the vibrant energy of New York after dark.

Chapter 44: Predicting Market Shifts: Being One Step Ahead

The city lights of New York shimmered outside, casting a soft glow inside Aanya 's car. The atmosphere was more relaxed, the weight of the day's learnings giving way to a more casual, laid-back vibe.

"So, Aanya," I began, adjusting the car's music to a softer tune, "What's your favorite genre of music?"

She glanced at me, a bit surprised by the shift in conversation. "Oh, I love pop and a bit of jazz. But lately, I've been into indie music. It's like discovering a hidden gem before it becomes mainstream."

I smiled, sensing an opportunity. "Ah, so you like being ahead of the curve, predicting the next big thing in music?"

She laughed, "I guess you could say that. It's fun to know about something before everyone else does."

"That's the essence of predicting market shifts in sales," I remarked casually. "Being able to anticipate what's going to be the next big thing, understanding trends, and positioning yourself accordingly."

Aanya looked intrigued, "Go on."

 "Well, think of it this way. Just like you enjoy discovering a song before it becomes a hit, in sales, we aim to identify potential market shifts. It's about reading the signs, understanding customer behavior, and then positioning our product or service in a way that it becomes the next big hit."

She pondered for a moment. "So, it's like being a trendsetter?"

"Exactly," I replied. "But it's not just about intuition. It's backed by data, research, and a deep understanding of the market. For instance, when streaming services were just starting, those who predicted its rise and adapted quickly are now industry leaders."

Aanya nodded, "Makes sense. But how do you stay one step ahead?"

I smiled, "By being curious, always learning, and not being afraid to take calculated risks. And by listening. Listening to the market, to customers, and even to competitors."

We continued our conversation, touching upon various topics - from her favorite travel destinations to her most memorable sales pitch. But throughout, I subtly wove in lessons on predicting market shifts, illustrating with anecdotes and examples.

As we neared the club, Aanya turned to me, her eyes sparkling with realization. "You did it again, didn't you? Teaching me without making it feel like a lesson."

I chuckled, "Guilty as charged. But that's the beauty of sales. It's everywhere, in every conversation, every interaction. And sometimes, the best lessons are the ones we don't even realize we're learning."

She smiled, "Well, here's to more 'unintentional' lessons then."And with that, we stepped out of the car, ready to enjoy the night, with the knowledge that every moment holds the potential for growth and learning.

Chapter 45: Reinventing the Sales Approach: Pivoting When Necessary

The club's atmosphere was electric. Neon lights danced across the room, and the pulsating beats of the music resonated with the energy of the crowd. Aanya led me through the throngs of people, introducing me to a group of her friends. Their warm greetings and lively chatter added to the evening's excitement.

As we settled into a plush seating area, Aanya signaled for a waiter. She had a specific request in mind, something that would make the evening even more special. However, the waiter seemed hesitant, explaining that what she was asking for wasn't part of their usual service.

I could sense Aanya 's disappointment. She had been looking forward to this particular experience. Not one to back down easily, I decided to step in. "May I have a word?" I asked the waiter, my tone polite yet firm.

He nodded, and we stepped aside. Drawing upon my years of sales experience, I began to negotiate. Instead of making demands, I started by understanding his perspective. "I understand that this isn't a usual request," I began, "but perhaps there's a way we can make it work?"

The waiter explained the challenges, and I listened intently. Then, using a technique I often employed in sales, I reframed the situation, highlighting the benefits for the club and suggesting a win-win solution.

After a few minutes of discussion, the waiter's demeanor changed. He seemed more open, even enthusiastic about the idea. "Let me check with my manager," he said, disappearing for a moment.

When he returned, he had good news. "We can make it happen," he announced, much to Aanya's delight.

As the evening progressed, I couldn't help but reflect on the importance of adaptability in sales. Just as I had pivoted my approach with the waiter, successful salespeople must be willing to reinvent their strategies when faced with challenges.

Golden Rule 1: "Adaptability is the key to sales success." - Brian Tracy, "The Psychology of Selling"

In the ever-changing world of sales, what worked yesterday might not work today. Being rigid in our approach can lead to missed opportunities.

Golden Rule 2: "Every no gets you closer to a yes." - Zig Ziglar, "Secrets of Closing the Sale"

Rejections are a part of sales. But instead of seeing them as setbacks, view them as opportunities to learn, adapt, and improve.

Golden Rule 3: "Change before you have to." - Jack Welch

In the fast-paced world of sales, waiting for change to happen can leave you behind. Proactively seek out new strategies and techniques to stay ahead of the curve.

As the night wore on, the club's energy never waned. And as we finally made our way out at 2 a.m., Aanya's friends couldn't stop raving about the evening, especially the special arrangement I had facilitated.

Walking along the streets of New York, the city lights illuminating our path, Aanya's friends expressed their gratitude. "You have a unique way of handling situations," one of them remarked.

I smiled, "It's all about understanding, adapting, and finding a way to make things work."

As we reached Aanya's car, the night's lessons lingered in the air. Sales, much like life, is about navigating challenges, reinventing our approach, and always striving for the best possible outcome.

Bonus Chapter: The Power of Personal Branding: Leaving a Lasting Impression

The city lights of New York shimmered outside the car window, casting a soft glow on the streets. The energy of the night still lingered, but the atmosphere inside the car was more relaxed, intimate even.

Aanya broke the silence, "You know, tonight was something else. I've never seen someone handle situations the way you do. It's like you have this... aura around you."

I chuckled, "It's not magic, Aanya. It's personal branding."

She looked intrigued, "Personal branding? Like celebrities and influencers?"

I nodded, "Exactly, but it's not just for them. Everyone has a personal brand, whether they realize it or not. It's how people perceive you, and what they think of when they hear your name. And in sales, it can make all the difference."

Aanya thought for a moment, "So, it's like your reputation?"

"Exactly," I replied. "Your personal brand is a combination of your actions, words, and even your appearance. It's how you present yourself to the world. And in sales, it can be a powerful tool. If clients trust and respect your personal brand, they're more likely to do business with you."

She seemed deep in thought, "So, how do you build a strong personal brand?"

I smiled, "It's a journey, not a destination. It starts with self-awareness, and understanding your strengths and weaknesses. Then, it's about consistency, and being authentic in all your interactions. And finally, it's about continuous learning and growth, always striving to be the best version of yourself."

Aanya looked inspired, "I never thought of it that way. But it makes so much sense. Especially in sales, where relationships are everything."

We pulled up to the hotel, and as I stepped out of the car, I turned to Aanya, "Remember, your personal brand is like a fingerprint, unique to you. Nurture it, protect it, and it can open doors you never even knew existed."

She nodded, her eyes shining with determination, "I will. Thank you for everything."

I smiled, "The pleasure was all mine. And remember, in the world of sales, your personal brand is your most valuable asset."

With that, I walked into the hotel, leaving Aanya with a newfound understanding of the power of personal branding.

Key Lessons and Golden Rules from Step 9: Adapting to Market Changes

1. Stay Informed: The healthcare landscape is ever-evolving. Regularly update your knowledge to stay relevant and competitive. Golden Rule: "Knowledge is power. Stay updated to stay ahead." - Reference: "The World is Flat" by Thomas L. Friedman
2. Embrace Innovation: The future of sales lies in leveraging new techniques and technologies. Golden Rule: "Innovate or stagnate." - Reference: "Innovator's Dilemma" by Clayton Christensen
3. Adaptability is Key: In a dynamic market, flexibility and adaptability are not just assets; they're necessities. Golden Rule: "The most adaptable survive." - Reference: "Who Moved My Cheese?" by Dr. Spencer Johnson
4. Empathy in Adaptation: Understand the changing needs and preferences of your customers. Adapt your strategies accordingly. Golden Rule: "Walk a mile in

your customer's shoes." - Reference: "How to Win Friends and Influence People" by Dale Carnegie

5. Anticipate Market Shifts: Always be on the lookout for signs of change in the market. Being proactive can give you a competitive edge. Golden Rule: "Forewarned is forearmed." - Reference: "The Art of Strategy" by Avinash K. Dixit & Barry J. Nalebuff

6. Reinvent When Necessary: Don't be afraid to pivot your sales approach if the situation demands it. Golden Rule: "Change is the only constant." - Reference: "The Lean Startup" by Eric Ries

7. Continuous Learning: The market, technology, and customer preferences change. Continuous learning ensures you're not left behind. Golden Rule: "Never stop learning." - Reference: "Lifelong Learning" by Albert Einstein

8. Build Relationships: In a changing market, strong relationships can provide stability and open doors to new opportunities. Golden Rule: "Business is all about relationships." - Reference: "Never Eat Alone" by Keith Ferrazzi

9. Feedback is Gold: Use feedback to understand market needs and adapt accordingly. Golden Rule: "Feedback is the breakfast of champions." - Reference: "Thanks for the Feedback" by Douglas Stone & Sheila Heen

10. Diversify: Don't put all your eggs in one basket. Diversifying product offerings can help navigate market changes. Golden Rule: "Diversification is a protection against ignorance." - Reference: "The Intelligent Investor" by Benjamin Graham

11. Stay Curious: A curious mindset can help you spot trends and opportunities before others do. Golden Rule:

"Curiosity is the engine of achievement." - Reference: "Curious" by Ian Leslie

12. Value Proposition: In a changing market, ensure your value proposition remains strong and relevant. Golden Rule: "Value is what people are willing to pay for." - Reference: "Value Proposition Design" by Alexander Osterwalder

13. Collaborate: Collaborate with others to gain different perspectives and insights into market changes. Golden Rule: "Alone we can do so little; together we can do so much." - Reference: "The Wisdom of Crowds" by James Surowiecki

14. Stay Agile: In a dynamic environment, an agile approach allows for quick adaptation and response to changes. Golden Rule: "Stay agile, stay ahead." - Reference: "Agile Estimating and Planning" by Mike Cohn

15. Trust Your Instincts: While data and research are vital, sometimes your gut feeling, based on experience, can guide you right. Golden Rule: "Trust your instincts, they are messages from your soul." - Reference: "Blink" by Malcolm Gladwell

Step 10: Building a Personal Brand

In the ever-evolving landscape of professional success and achievement, one aspect remains constant - the undeniable influence of a personal brand. As we delve into "Step 10: Building a Personal Brand," we enter a realm where individuality and authenticity reign supreme.

In today's crowded and competitive arena, having a personal brand is no longer a luxury; it's a necessity. It's the distinctive imprint you leave on your field, a reflection of your values, expertise, and unique journey. It's the unspoken promise you make to your audience - the commitment to stand out and deliver excellence.

This step is your guide to harnessing the immense power of personal branding. We'll explore the art of crafting an image that not only stands out but leaves an indelible mark. We'll draw inspiration from real-world journeys, such as that of Dr. Vijay Viraj, who has paved his own path to personal branding success.

But building a personal brand isn't merely about image; it's about connection. We'll delve into the intricacies of engaging with your audience, building a loyal following that believes in your message and vision.

In an era defined by digital presence, we'll explore the myriad ways to leverage online platforms, using the digital realm as a canvas to paint your personal brand. We'll delve into the tools, strategies, and practices that ensure your brand's voice is heard loud and clear.

And as we venture further, we'll emphasize the cornerstone of it all - consistency. Maintaining a cohesive image, a promise delivered day after day, is what cements your brand in the hearts and minds of your audience.

So, get ready to embark on this transformative journey. Step 10 isn't just about building a personal brand; it's about crafting your legacy, one authentic step at a time. Welcome to the world of personal branding.

Chapter 46: The Power of Personal Branding: Standing Out in a Crowded Field

The day began with an unexpected call from Aanya. Her voice, filled with excitement, hinted at a surprise. "Get ready quickly, Dr. Vijay, and skip the hotel breakfast. I have something special planned for today," she said. Intrigued, I quickly prepared myself for the day ahead.

As I stepped out of the hotel, Aanya was already there, waiting in her car. We drove out of the bustling city, and after a while, the scenery began to change. The cacophony of New York was replaced by the harmonious sounds of nature. Before I knew it, we had arrived at a serene resort, its entrance adorned with lush greenery and the soft melodies of chirping birds.

The resort's ambiance was immediately captivating. It wasn't just another luxury resort; it had a unique identity and a distinct brand that set it apart from the rest. As we walked in, we were greeted with a welcome drink, a special concoction that the resort was known for.

Raising her glass, Aanya initiated our discussion. "This resort, Dr. Vijay, stands out, doesn't it? Just like how a strong personal brand should."

I nodded in agreement. "Absolutely, Aanya. Just as this resort has carved a niche for itself amidst numerous others, individuals too must create a unique brand identity to stand out in a crowded field."

Golden Rule: "Your brand is what people say about you when you're not in the room." - Jeff Bezos, Founder of Amazon. It's essential to ensure that what they say aligns with the brand image you want to project.

As we sipped our drinks, I elaborated, "In today's digital age, with the proliferation of social media, personal branding has become more crucial than ever. It's not just about self-promotion but about establishing a reputation, building trust, and positioning oneself as an authority in one's field."

Aanya looked thoughtful. "So, how does one go about building such a brand?"

Golden Rule: "Start by knowing what you want and who you are, build credibility around it and deliver it online in a compelling way." - Krista Neher, CEO of Boot Camp Digital. It's about authenticity and consistency.

I pointed towards the resort. "Look around. This resort didn't just happen overnight. They identified what they wanted to be known for, built their services around it, and consistently delivered exceptional experiences. Similarly, personal branding is a journey. It requires self-awareness, a clear vision, and consistent efforts."

Fact: According to a study by CareerBuilder, 70% of employers use social media to screen candidates. A strong personal brand can significantly influence potential employers or clients.

Aanya jotted down notes, and her dedication was evident. "So, it's about creating a unique identity, being authentic, and consistently delivering value?"

Golden Rule: "To be in business today, our most important job is to be head marketer for the brand called You" - Tom Peters, Author of "The Brand You 50". Every interaction, online or offline, contributes to your personal brand.

I smiled, "Exactly. And remember, it's an ongoing process. The world is ever-evolving, and so should your brand."

As we finished our drinks, I could see Aanya's mind buzzing with ideas. The resort, with its distinct brand, had provided the perfect backdrop for our discussion on personal branding. And this was just the beginning of our day.

Chapter 47: Crafting the Sales Lion Image: Dr. Vijay Viraj's Branding Journey

The sun was now higher in the sky, casting a warm glow over the resort. Aanya and I decided to explore the amenities, starting with the pristine pool. The pool, with its clear blue waters, seemed inviting, and around it were guests lounging, some reading, others simply soaking in the sun.

As we walked, I began, "Aanya, this pool reminds me of the early days of my career. Just like this clear water, I had clarity of purpose but was unsure of the depth I could reach."

She looked at me, intrigued, "Go on..."

Golden Rule: "Your personal brand is a promise to your clients... a promise of quality, consistency, competency, and reliability." - Jason Hartman, CEO of Platinum Properties Investor Network.

Just like this pool promises relaxation and rejuvenation, your brand should deliver on its promises.

I continued, "In the initial days, I was known for my sales skills, but I wanted to be more than just a salesperson. I wanted to be a thought leader, a guide, a mentor. That's when the 'Sales Lion' image started taking shape."

We moved from the pool area to the beautifully manicured gardens, filled with exotic plants and flowers. "These gardens," I said, "represent the growth and nurturing of my brand. Just as these plants need care, my brand needed nurturing, learning, and evolving."

Fact: According to Forbes, 33% of all buyers trust the brand, while 90% trust product or service recommendations from peers. Building a personal brand can significantly boost trust and credibility.

Aanya, taking in the beauty around her, reflected, "I've been so focused on sales numbers and targets that I've never really thought about my personal brand. But seeing your journey and this resort's unique identity, I realize the importance."

Golden Rule: "People do not buy goods and services. They buy relations, stories, and magic." - Seth Godin, Author and Entrepreneur. Your brand story is your magic.

She then asked, "How did you ensure that your brand remained consistent over the years?"

I smiled, "It's about staying true to your core values while adapting to the changing environment. Just like this resort, which maintains its essence while offering modern amenities."

As we concluded our tour of the gardens, Aanya seemed deep in thought. "Your journey, Dr. Vijay, is truly inspiring. It makes me want to start crafting my own brand story."

I nodded, "And that's the first step, Aanya. Recognizing the need and then taking action."

As we headed back, the resort had already given us so much to reflect upon. Little did we know, the day had more insights in store for us.

Chapter 48: Engaging with Your Audience: Building a Loyal Following

The sun was now at its zenith, casting shimmering reflections on the water. Aanya and I decided to head to the resort's private beach. The soft sand under our feet and the rhythmic sound of the waves created a tranquil atmosphere.

As we settled on the sun loungers, Aanya remarked, "This beach, with its exclusivity, reminds me of how brands create a loyal customer base. It's not just about attracting people; it's about making them stay."

I nodded in agreement, "Exactly, Aanya. Engaging with your audience is crucial. It's not just about making a sale; it's about building a relationship."

Golden Rule: "Your brand is what other people say about you when you're not in the room." - Jeff Bezos, Founder of Amazon. Engaging with your audience ensures that they speak positively about you.

I continued, "In today's digital age, it's easier than ever to connect with your audience. Social media, webinars, podcasts... the avenues are endless."

Fact: According to HubSpot, 64% of marketers actively invest time in search engine optimization (SEO) to engage with their audience. Additionally, 70% of marketers are actively investing in content marketing to drive engagement.

Aanya looked thoughtful, "But with so many platforms, how do you ensure consistent engagement?"

Golden Rule: "Content builds relationships. Relationships are built on trust. Trust drives revenue." - Andrew Davis, Bestselling Author and Keynote Speaker. Offer value to your audience, and they'll keep coming back.

I replied, "It's about understanding your audience's needs and preferences. For instance, if your audience is more active on LinkedIn, focus your efforts there. Share valuable content, respond to comments, and actively participate in discussions."

Aanya, looking at the vast expanse of the ocean, said, "It's like these waves. They keep coming back to the shore, no matter how many times they recede."

I smiled, "A perfect analogy, Aanya. Your audience will keep coming back if you give them a reason to."

As the afternoon sun began its descent, we realized how time had flown. The beach, with its endless horizon, had given us a perspective on the limitless possibilities of engaging with an audience. And as we headed back to the resort, we were both eager to explore the next chapter of our journey.

Chapter 49: Leveraging Digital Platforms: Online Branding Strategies

After the enlightening discussion at the beach, we decided to head to the resort's tech lounge, a space equipped with the latest gadgets and high-speed internet. The contrast was evident - from the natural serenity of the beach to the buzzing digital world.

As we settled into the comfortable chairs, Aanya pulled out her tablet. "You know, Dr. Vijay, I've been trying to establish my online presence, but it's so overwhelming with all these platforms."

I nodded, understanding her dilemma. "The digital world is vast, but it's also where most of our audience spends their time. Leveraging these platforms effectively can skyrocket your personal brand."

Golden Rule: "Engage, Enlighten, Encourage and especially...just be yourself! Social media is a community effort; everyone is an asset." - Susan Cooper, Digital Marketer and Influencer. Authenticity is key in the digital realm.

Fact: According to Datareportal, more than 4.5 billion people now use the internet, with social media users passing the 3.8 billion mark. This highlights the immense potential of digital platforms.

Aanya looked intrigued, "But how do you decide which platform to focus on?"

I replied, "It's essential to know where your target audience hangs out. For B2B, platforms like LinkedIn are gold. For B2C, Instagram or Facebook might be more effective."

Golden Rule: "Content is fire; social media is gasoline." - Jay Baer, Digital Marketing Consultant and Speaker. Use social media to amplify your content.

Aanya then asked, "What about consistency?"

I smiled, "Consistency is the key. Regular updates, posts, and engagement can boost your visibility exponentially. But remember, it's not just about quantity but quality."

Fact: According to the Content Marketing Institute, 90% of top-performing B2B content marketers prioritize the audience's informational needs over their promotional message.

Golden Rule: "People want to do business with you because you help them get what they want. They don't do business with you to help you get what you want." - Don Crowther, Social Media Marketing Expert. Always prioritize your audience's needs.

As we wrapped up our discussion, the lounge's ambiance, with its blend of technology and comfort, served as a reminder of the digital era's potential. Aanya seemed more confident, ready to dive into the digital world and make her mark.

Chapter 50: Consistency in Branding: Maintaining a Cohesive Image

The sun began its descent, casting a warm, golden hue over the resort. Aanya, ever the curious learner, led us to the resort's renowned art gallery. The entrance was adorned with a beautiful mosaic that shimmered in the evening light, hinting at the treasures inside.

As we stepped in, the vast expanse of the gallery was filled with a harmonious arrangement of paintings, sculptures, and installations. Each artwork, while distinct in its essence, seemed to resonate with a consistent theme, echoing the resort's brand identity.

Aanya, pausing to admire a series of paintings, remarked, "These paintings, though from different eras and styles, seem to have a common thread running through them. It's as if they're telling a continuous story."

I nodded in agreement, "That's an astute observation. Just like these paintings, branding requires a harmonious blend of consistency and uniqueness. While every campaign or strategy might differ, they should all align with your brand's core values and image."

Golden Rule: "Consistency is the DNA of mastery." - Robin Sharma, Leadership Expert and Author. This principle is paramount in branding.

Fact: Lucidpress states that consistent brand presentation across all platforms can increase revenue by up to 23%.

"Think of branding as a symphony," I elaborated. "Each instrument plays a different tune, but together they create a harmonious melody. Similarly, every aspect of your brand, from your logo to your customer service, should resonate with your brand's core essence."

Aanya looked thoughtful, "So, it's not just about having a catchy slogan or a memorable logo. It's about ensuring that every interaction, every touchpoint with the customer, reflects the brand's promise."

"Exactly," I replied. "Your brand voice, visuals, and even the way you handle customer complaints should be consistent. It's this consistency that builds trust and makes your brand recognizable."

Fact: Nielsen's study reveals that 59% of consumers prefer to buy new products from brands familiar to them.

Golden Rule: "Your brand is the single most important investment you can make in your business." - Steve Forbes, Chairman and Editor-in-Chief of Forbes Media.

As we meandered through the gallery, Aanya stopped in front of a contemporary art piece. "This is different from the others, yet it feels like it belongs here. Is that what you mean by consistency in branding?"

I smiled, "Precisely. It's about evolving without losing your essence. Just as this piece brings a fresh perspective to the gallery while staying true to its theme, brands should innovate while remaining consistent with their core identity."

Golden Rule "Your brand is a story unfolding across all customer touchpoints." - Jonah Sachs, Author and Entrepreneur.

Our tour of the gallery culminated with a deeper understanding of the importance of consistency in branding. As we exited, the gallery's embodiment of a cohesive brand image served as a lasting impression, emphasizing that branding is not just about logos or slogans but an integrated, consistent approach to every facet of a brand.

Key Learnings and Golden Rules from Step 10: Building a Personal Brand

1. Branding is Perception: How people perceive you or your product is the essence of branding. It's not just about a logo or a catchy slogan; it's the emotion and thought that arises when someone hears your name.

2. Golden Rule #1: "Your brand is what other people say about you when you're not in the room." - Jeff Bezos, Founder of Amazon.
3. Stay Updated: In a rapidly changing world, especially in sectors like healthcare, it's crucial to stay updated with the latest trends and shifts to maintain a relevant brand image.
4. Golden Rule #2: "Innovation distinguishes between a leader and a follower." - Steve Jobs, Co-founder of Apple Inc..
5. Embrace Innovation: In the digital age, embracing new techniques and technologies is not just beneficial; it's essential. It can set you apart from competitors and offer a unique selling proposition.
6. Golden Rule #3: "The best way to predict the future is to create it." - Peter Drucker, Management Consultant and Author.
7. Adaptability is Key: The ability to adapt to changing circumstances, be it market shifts or personal challenges, is a hallmark of successful individuals and brands.
8. Golden Rule #4: "It is not the strongest of the species that survive, nor the most intelligent, but the one most responsive to change." - Charles Darwin, Naturalist and Geologist.
9. Anticipate Market Shifts: Being proactive rather than reactive to market changes can give you a competitive edge. It's about reading the signs and making informed predictions.
10. Golden Rule #5: "Change before you have to." - Jack Welch, Former CEO of General Electric.

11. Reinvent but Stay True: While it's essential to evolve and reinvent your strategies, staying true to your brand's core values ensures authenticity.
12. Golden Rule #6: "Your premium brand had better be delivering something special, or it's not going to get the business." - Warren Buffett, Investor and Philanthropist.
13. Consistency Builds Trust: A consistent brand image across all touchpoints, from customer service to marketing campaigns, builds trust and loyalty.
14. Golden Rule #7: "Consistency is the DNA of mastery." - Robin Sharma, Leadership Expert and Author.
15. Invest in Your Brand: Your brand is an asset. Investing time, effort, and resources into building and maintaining it can yield significant returns.
16. Golden Rule #8: "Your brand is the single most important investment you can make in your business." - Steve Forbes, Chairman and Editor-in-Chief of Forbes Media.
17. Engage with Your Audience: Building a loyal following is about engagement. It's about two-way communication, understanding their needs, and delivering value.
18. Golden Rule #9: "Your brand is a story unfolding across all customer touchpoints." - Jonah Sachs, Author and Entrepreneur.
19. Leverage Digital Platforms: In today's digital age, online branding strategies, from social media to content marketing, are indispensable.
20. Golden Rule #10: "Branding demands commitment; commitment to continual re-invention." - Richard Branson, Founder of Virgin Group.

Step 11: Ethics and Integrity in Sales

In the realm of sales, where strategies and approaches can vary widely, there's one foundation that should never waver - ethics and integrity. "Step 11: Ethics and Integrity in Sales" is a vital juncture in our journey, underscoring the pivotal role that moral values and honesty play in the world of commerce.

This step is a compass that guides us through the intricacies of ethical decision-making. It's a reminder that while success in sales can be measured in various ways, the true measure of a salesperson lies in their moral compass.

Throughout these subchapters, we'll delve into the intricate path of ethical dilemmas and the principles that guide us. "The

Moral Compass: Navigating Ethical Dilemmas" will help us discern right from wrong in the complex landscape of sales.

We'll then explore "The Sales Lion's Code of Conduct," an unspoken creed that distinguishes those who sell with integrity. Building trust is the cornerstone of ethical sales, and "Building Trust through Transparency: Honesty in Sales" sheds light on the value of openness in every interaction.

Inevitably, ethical challenges arise in the dynamic world of sales. "Handling Ethical Challenges: Case Studies and Reflections" invites us to reflect on real-world scenarios, learning from the experiences of others.

And as we look beyond the immediate horizon, we'll discuss "The Long-Term Impact of Ethical Sales." Here, we'll discover how ethical practices not only build a lasting legacy for a salesperson but also contribute to a thriving, ethical business environment.

So, as we venture into Step 11, remember that integrity is the currency of trust in sales. It's about more than the bottom line; it's about a reputation that transcends transactions and a legacy built on unwavering principles. Welcome to the world of ethics and integrity in sales.

Chapter 51: The Moral Compass: Navigating Ethical Dilemmas

Late evening by the resort's fireplace, the crackling flames were casting a warm glow on the surroundings. The ambiance was serene, with the distant sound of crickets and the gentle rustling of leaves.

Aanya, her cheeks slightly flushed from the wine, leaned in closer, her voice a soft whisper. "Dr. Vijay, there have been times in my sales career when I've been tempted to take shortcuts, to make a deal happen. How do you always seem to do the right thing, even when no one's watching?"

Dr. Vijay looked deep into the flames, collecting his thoughts. "Aanya," he began, "life and sales are filled with choices. Every decision we make, no matter how insignificant it might seem, reflects our character. It's like a compass that guides us."

Golden Rule: "In the words of Stephen R. Covey in 'The 7 Habits of Highly Effective People', 'Our character is basically a composite of our habits.' It's essential to cultivate habits that align with ethical principles."

Aanya pondered this, swirling the wine in her glass. "But what if an unethical choice could lead to a significant sale? Or if everyone else is doing it?"

Dr. Vijay nodded, understanding her dilemma. "It's easy to justify a choice by looking at immediate gains or comparing ourselves to others. But in the long run, those choices catch up with us."

Golden Rule: As Warren Buffet once said, 'It takes 20 years to build a reputation and five minutes to ruin it. If you think about that, you'll do things differently.' Every decision impacts our reputation, and in sales, reputation is everything."

Aanya looked thoughtful. "I remember a deal where I could have easily misled a client for a quick sale. I was so tempted, especially with the pressure from my team. But something held me back."

"That's your moral compass, Aanya," Dr. Vijay responded. "It's that inner voice that guides you, even when the path isn't clear."

Fact: According to a survey by Santa Clara University, 49% of employees have been pressured by their superiors to act unethically to achieve company goals. Yet, companies with a strong ethical identity tend to outperform others.

Aanya sighed, "But it's hard, especially when you see others succeeding by taking those shortcuts."

Dr. Vijay placed a reassuring hand on her shoulder. "Short-term gains can lead to long-term losses. Ethical decisions might not always bring immediate rewards, but they build trust, loyalty, and a legacy."

Golden Rule: As Robert Brault aptly put it, 'There is no higher value in our society than integrity.' It's the cornerstone of all interactions, personal or professional."

The two sat in reflective silence, the weight of the conversation sinking in. The fire's warmth, the serene environment, and the depth of their discussion made for a profound moment of connection and understanding.

As the evening drew to a close, Aanya felt a renewed sense of purpose. She realized that her moral compass, her ethical principles, would be her guiding light in the complex world of sales. And with mentors like Dr. Vijay, she felt equipped to navigate any challenge that came her way.

Chapter 52: The Sales Lion's Code of Conduct: Selling with Integrity

The crackling flames of the resort's bonfire cast a warm, orange glow, and the stars above shimmered brilliantly. The ambiance was intimate, with just the two of us seated comfortably, each holding a glass of wine.

Aanya took a deep breath, her face reflecting the fire's glow. "Dr. Vijay," she began hesitantly, "I want to apologize for earlier. I got carried away by the moment and my emotions."

Dr. Vijay raised his hand gently, "Aanya, there's no need to apologize. We all have moments of vulnerability. What's important is how we handle them and move forward."

She looked relieved, "Thank you for understanding. It's just that I've learned so much from you, and sometimes emotions get the better of me."

Dr. Vijay sipped his wine thoughtfully, "Speaking of learning, let's discuss something that's been the cornerstone of my career - my personal 'Code of Conduct' in sales."

Aanya leaned in, eager to hear more. "Tell me about it."

Golden Rule: "Warren Buffet once said, 'It takes 20 years to build a reputation and five minutes to ruin it.' This has always resonated with me. Integrity is the foundation of all successful sales."

Aanya nodded, taking a moment to let that sink in. "So, what's the first principle of your code?"

Dr. Vijay replied, "Always prioritize the client's needs. Even if it means losing a sale. In the long run, trust and credibility are more valuable than any single transaction."

Fact: A survey by HubSpot found that 82% of consumers consider trustworthiness as the most crucial trait in their decision-making process.

Aanya looked thoughtful, "That's a powerful principle. What else?"

Dr. Vijay continued, "Secondly, always be transparent. If a product or service isn't right for the client, be upfront about it. Honesty fosters trust."

Golden Rule: As Stephen R. Covey stated, "Trust is the glue of life. It's the most essential ingredient in effective communication." Building trust is paramount in sales.

Aanya took a sip of her wine, "And what if you're faced with a situation where there's a gray area, ethically speaking?"

Dr. Vijay looked into the fire, "That's where the third principle comes in. When in doubt, refer back to your code. If a decision doesn't align with your core values, it's probably not the right one."

Fact: According to the Ethics & Compliance Initiative, companies with a strong ethical culture outperform their counterparts by 16% in terms of profitability.

Golden Rule: As Albert Einstein wisely said, "Relativity applies to physics, not ethics." There's no gray area when it comes to doing the right thing.

The night deepened, and the fire's warmth enveloped them. Aanya felt a renewed sense of purpose and clarity. As they finished their wine, she realized that the true essence of sales lay not just in closing deals but in building relationships anchored in trust, respect, and integrity.

Chapter 53: Building Trust through Transparency: Honesty in Sales

After finishing the wine, we decided to walk in the resort's garden. The garden was bathed in soft moonlight. The fragrance of blooming flowers filled the air, and the gentle sound of water from a nearby fountain created a tranquil ambiance. I and Aanya stroll leisurely, the gravel crunching softly under their feet.

Aanya took a deep breath, inhaling the fresh scent of the flowers. "This place is magical, Dr. Vijay. It's so peaceful."

Dr. Vijay nodded, "It's the perfect setting to reflect and share. Speaking of which, have you ever faced a situation in sales where being completely honest might cost you the deal?"

Aanya hesitated, "Well, I've always tried to be honest, but sometimes I wonder if it's worth it. Especially when I see others bending the truth a bit and making the sale."

Dr. Vijay looked at her thoughtfully, "Let me share a story from my early days in sales." He began, "I was pitching a dental product to a large clinic. During the presentation, I realized that while our product was top-notch, it might not be the best fit for that specific clinic due to their unique requirements."

Aanya's eyes widened, "That sounds like a tough spot. What did you do?"

"I was transparent about it," Dr. Vijay replied. "I told them that while our product was excellent, another product in the market might serve their specific needs better."

Aanya looked puzzled, "But why? You could have just kept quiet and made the sale."

Dr. Vijay smiled gently, "True, but then I would have lost something far more valuable than a sale – my integrity."

Golden Rule: As Mark Twain wisely said, "Honesty is the best policy. If I lose my honor, I lose myself." Honesty might sometimes cost a sale, but it always wins respect.

Fact: A study by Label Insight found that 94% of consumers are likely to be loyal to a brand that offers complete transparency.

Aanya pondered this, "So, you're saying that even if honesty costs in the short term, it pays off in the long run?"

"Exactly," Dr. Vijay affirmed. "Trust is like a currency in sales. Once you devalue it, it's tough to regain its worth. And in that instance, the clinic's head was so impressed with my honesty that he referred me to three other clinics. I ended up closing much larger deals with them."

Golden Rule: Zig Ziglar once remarked, "If people like you, they'll listen to you, but if they trust you, they'll do business with you." Trust is the bedrock of lasting business relationships.

Fact: According to Edelman's Trust Barometer, 81% of consumers say that the ability to trust the brand is a deal-breaker or a deciding factor in their buying decision.

Aanya looked thoughtful, "I've always believed in honesty, but hearing your experiences reinforces that belief. It's not just about making a sale; it's about building a relationship."

Dr. Vijay nodded, "Exactly. And relationships built on trust and honesty stand the test of time."

As they continued their walk, the conversation flowed naturally, touching upon various aspects of sales, ethics, and life values. By the time they reached the end of the garden path, Aanya felt a renewed sense of purpose and clarity.

Chapter 54: Handling Ethical Challenges: Case Studies and Reflections

Noticing Aanya's slightly unsteady demeanor, possibly from the wine, I gently suggested, "Let's sit by the pool, Aanya. The water might help you feel better." As they approached the resort's pool, it shimmered invitingly under the moonlight. The tranquil atmosphere was palpable, and the water's calmness seemed to mirror the serenity around them. They settled by the poolside, dipping their feet into the cool embrace of the water, sending gentle ripples across its surface.

Aanya sighed, "You know, Dr. Vijay, your stories have been so enlightening. But I've faced some ethical challenges in my sales career that left me perplexed."

Dr. Vijay looked at her, encouraging her to continue. "Please share, Aanya . Reflection is the first step towards understanding."

She hesitated for a moment, then began, "Once, I was selling a dental product, and I overheard a competitor bad-mouthing our product to a potential client. I was tempted to retaliate by doing the same about their product. But I held back. Was that the right thing to do?"

Dr. Vijay nodded, "Absolutely. Retaliating would have dragged you down to their level. Instead, focusing on the strengths of your product and building trust with your client is the ethical way."

Golden Rule: "Your beliefs become your thoughts. Your thoughts become your words. Your words become your actions. Your actions become your habits. Your habits become your values. Your values become your destiny."- Mahatma Gandhi

This quote underscores the idea that a person's character and reputation are shaped by their consistent ethical choices over time.

Fact: According to a survey by the Ethics & Compliance Initiative, companies with a strong ethical culture outperform their counterparts by 13% in terms of productivity.

Aanya looked relieved, "I'm glad I made the right choice. But there was another instance where a client was misinformed about our product's capabilities. I had the chance to close the deal based on that misinformation. I chose to correct them, even if it meant losing the sale."

Dr. Vijay smiled, "That's commendable. Ethical challenges test our character. By choosing the right path, you not only upheld your integrity but also built trust."

Golden Rule: As Dale Carnegie mentioned, "You can make more friends in two months by becoming interested in other people than you can in two years by trying to get other people interested in you." Genuine interest and honesty always pay off.

Fact: A study by the CFA Institute found that 71% of investors value a financial firm's ethical conduct over its financial returns.

Aanya leaned back, looking at the stars, "But it's not always easy. Sometimes the line between right and wrong is blurred."

Dr. Vijay agreed, "True. That's why it's essential to have a strong moral compass and reflect on our actions regularly."

They continued discussing various case studies, each presenting its own set of ethical challenges. Dr. Vijay shared his insights, emphasizing the importance of ethical decision-making in building a lasting legacy in sales.

Golden Rule: As Stephen R. Covey stated in 'The 7 Habits of Highly Effective People', "Begin with the end in mind." Always consider the long-term impact of your decisions.

As the night deepened, the reflections in the pool became clearer, mirroring their introspective conversation. The calmness of the water resonated with the clarity they both felt, understanding the profound impact of ethics in sales.

Chapter 55: The Long-Term Impact of Ethical Sales: Building a Lasting Legacy

The gentle sounds of water lapping at the pool's edge created a soothing backdrop for their conversation. Aanya, feeling the calming effects of the water, took a deep breath and said, "Dr. Vijay, I've always admired how you've built such a strong reputation in the industry. It's not just about the sales numbers, but the legacy you're leaving behind."

Dr. Vijay smiled, "Thank you, Aanya. But it's essential to understand that a legacy isn't built overnight. It's the culmination of consistent ethical decisions, even when they're hard."

Aanya looked thoughtful, "But how do you measure the impact of those decisions?"

Dr. Vijay responded, "It's in the trust you build, the relationships you nurture, and the reputation you create. When you prioritize ethics, you're not just thinking about the immediate sale. You're considering the long-term relationship with the client and the broader impact on society."

Golden Rule: "In sales, as in life, integrity is not a tactic but a philosophy." - Reference: "Integrity Selling for the 21st Century" by Ron Willingham

Aanya pondered this, "But surely, there must have been times when being ethical might have cost you a deal?"

Dr. Vijay nodded, "Absolutely. But those moments became the foundation of my brand. Clients knew that if I recommended something, it was in their best interest. That trustworthiness opened doors that no sales tactic ever could."

Golden Rule: "Trust is the most important currency in business. It's earned over time and can be lost in an instant." - Reference: "The Speed of Trust" by Stephen M.R. Covey

They sat in silence for a moment, the weight of the conversation sinking in. Aanya finally spoke, "I want to be remembered as someone who made a difference, not just someone who made sales."

Dr. Vijay smiled warmly, "And you will, Aanya. Just remember that every decision you make, every deal you close, contributes to the legacy you're building."

Golden Rule: "Your legacy is built on the choices you make, not the deals you close." - Reference: "Legacy: What the All Blacks Can Teach Us About the Business of Life" by James Kerr

As the night deepened, we continued to discuss the broader implications of the work, understanding that sales weren't just about numbers but about the impact we left on the world.

As we stood up to leave, Aanya, perhaps overwhelmed by the emotions of the night and the wine, lost her balance. My reflexes were quick, and he caught her before she could fall.

In that vulnerable moment, Aanya, looking into Dr. Vijay's eyes, was overcome with emotion and leaned in, attempting to bridge the distance between them. But Dr. Vijay, ever the embodiment of integrity, gently held her back.

"Aanya," he began softly, "I deeply value our bond and the trust we've built. But it's essential for both of us to remember the foundation of that trust – respect and integrity. Just as in sales, in life, we must always act with character, even when faced with challenging situations."

Aanya, her eyes glistening with tears, nodded, "I'm so sorry, Dr. Vijay. It's just... everything we've discussed, the wisdom you've shared, it's been overwhelming."

Dr. Vijay smiled kindly, "It's okay, Aanya. Emotions can sometimes cloud our judgment. But remember, our character is defined by how we act in those moments of vulnerability. Just as in sales, where we must uphold our integrity even when it's tempting to take shortcuts, in life, we must always choose the path that aligns with our core values."

Golden Rule: "Character is doing the right thing when nobody's looking." - Reference: "Good to Great" by Jim Collins

The night ends with Aanya expressing gratitude for the invaluable lessons. She understands that her feelings were a result of deep admiration and respect for Dr. Vijay's wisdom and character. They both agree to cherish this mentor-mentee bond, built on trust, respect, and shared values. With a final nod of understanding, they headed to their respective rooms in the resort, the silence of the night echoing the profound lessons of the evening.

Key Learnings and Golden Rules from Step 11: Ethics and Integrity in Sales

1. Always Prioritize Ethics: No matter the situation, always act with integrity and prioritize ethical considerations above all else.
2. Personal Values Guide Professional Actions: Your personal moral compass should guide your professional decisions. If something feels wrong personally, it's likely wrong professionally too.
3. The Sales Lion's Principle: Always sell with integrity, even if it means losing a sale. The trust you build is more valuable than any single transaction.
4. Transparency is Key: Always be honest with your clients. This builds trust, which is the foundation of any long-term business relationship.
5. Ethical Challenges are Growth Opportunities: When faced with an ethical dilemma, view it as an opportunity to reinforce your values and grow as a professional.
6. Reflect on Ethical Decisions: Regularly reflect on your decisions to ensure you're acting in line with your values and the best interests of your clients.
7. Trust, Once Lost, is Hard to Regain: It takes years to build trust and only a moment to lose it. Always act in a way that preserves and strengthens trust.

8. The Long-Term Impact: Ethical sales practices lead to lasting business relationships, repeat business, and positive word-of-mouth referrals.
9. Consistent Ethical Standards: Regardless of the client or the size of the deal, maintain consistent ethical standards in every transaction.
10. Learn from Mistakes: If you make an ethical misstep, acknowledge it, learn from it, and take steps to ensure it doesn't happen again.
11. The Sales Lion's Code: Develop a personal code of conduct that outlines your ethical standards and refer to it regularly.
12. Case Studies as Learning Tools: Regularly review and discuss ethical case studies to sharpen your decision-making skills.
13. Honesty Leads to Loyalty: Clients are more likely to remain loyal to salespeople who are honest, even when it's not in their immediate best interest.
14. Ethical Sales = Sustainable Business: Ethical sales practices lead to sustainable business growth and a positive brand reputation.
15. Legacy Building: Acting with integrity in sales not only benefits you in the short term but also contributes to building a lasting legacy in the industry.
16. Client's Best Interest: Always act in the best interest of the client, even if it means recommending a competitor's product.
17. Continuous Learning: The field of ethics is ever-evolving. Engage in continuous learning to stay updated on best practices and ethical considerations in sales.

Step 12: The Unexpected Opportunity: Leveraging Sales Expertise

In the journey of sales, where adaptability and expertise are your faithful companions, "Step 12: The Unexpected Opportunity" unveils a realm where unforeseen possibilities become stepping stones to success.

Here, we step into uncharted territory where every call, every interaction, and every challenge is an unexpected opportunity waiting to be seized. It's a chapter that unveils the hidden gems within the intricate world of sales, those moments where your sales expertise truly shines.

"The Surprise Call: Seizing New Opportunities" is our first stop on this enlightening journey. It showcases the art of recognizing unexpected opportunities and harnessing them to your advantage. This is where sales acumen meets serendipity.

Navigating the complex web of corporate dynamics is an essential skill for any salesperson. "First Impressions: Navigating Corporate Dynamics" delves into the intricacies of making a lasting impact and forging meaningful connections with key players.

Our voyage also includes "Tailored Training: Meeting Specific Needs," where we discover how personalized approaches not only meet clients' unique requirements but also transform challenges into triumphs.

Sales is full of twists and turns, and "Unveiling Surprises: The Unexpected Turn of Events" teaches us how to gracefully adapt to the unexpected and turn surprises into opportunities.

Finally, "The Journey of Discovery: From Skepticism to Admiration" takes us on a path where initial skepticism can evolve into admiration, opening doors we never expected.

In "Step 12," we celebrate the resilience, adaptability, and expertise that set sales professionals apart. Here, every twist and turn is an invitation to leverage your expertise, making the unexpected your greatest ally. Welcome to the world of the unexpected opportunity.

Chapter 56: The Surprise Call: Seizing New Opportunities Setting

The sun was casting its early morning glow over the New York skyline as Aanya and I drove back to the city from the resort. The tranquility of the past day still lingered in the air, creating a stark contrast to the bustling streets of Manhattan.

"Aanya," I began, "I must say, these past few days have been enlightening. Your thirst for knowledge, your dedication, it's truly commendable."

She smiled, her eyes reflecting gratitude. "Thank you. It's not every day you get to learn from the Sales Lion himself."

As we approached the hotel, Aanya's phone buzzed. Glancing at the screen, her expression shifted to one of urgency. "I have a meeting with a potential client. I need to rush. But thank you for everything," she said, pulling over.

I nodded, "All the best, Aanya. And thank you for being such a wonderful host and guide."

As I stepped out of the car, I couldn't help but admire Aanya's drive. Little did I know that her influence would soon open another door for me.

Back in my hotel room, amidst the sounds of New York's bustling streets, I began packing my bags. The memories of the past few days played in my mind when suddenly, my phone rang. The caller ID displayed an unknown number.

"Hello?"

"Is this the Dr Vijay Viraj?" a confident voice inquired.

"Yes, speaking."

"Hello. I'm Rajan, VP of the Learning and Development division at Ziva Corp. Aanya spoke highly of you, and we're interested in having you conduct a special training session for our sales team. Would you be available today for a 3-hour session?"

I was taken aback. I had plans to fly back to India the next day. But then, I remembered a golden rule from 'Networking for Success' by Richard Denny: "Opportunities don't happen. You create them."

"I can adjust my plans. Tell me more about what you're looking for," I responded.

As Rajan outlined the company's needs, I realized the importance of always being prepared. I recalled a statistic from **'The Networking Survival Guide'** by Diane Darling: "85% of all jobs are filled through networking." This wasn't a job, but the principle remained the same.

After finalizing the details, I tried calling Aanya to thank her for the reference, but her phone was switched off. I smiled, thinking of how interconnected the world of sales was.

As I prepared my notes for the training, I reflected on another golden rule from **'Never Eat Alone'** by Keith Ferrazzi: "Success in any field, but especially in business, is about working with people, not against them." Aanya's reference was a testament to that.

I knew that this unexpected opportunity was not just about imparting knowledge but also about showcasing the power of networking, seizing opportunities, and the importance of always being prepared.

I took a deep breath, ready to embrace this new challenge, reminding myself of the words of Zig Ziglar: "You don't have to be great to start, but you have to start to be great."

Chapter 57: First Impressions: Navigating Corporate Dynamics

The sleek glass facade of the company's headquarters towered above me, reflecting the bustling cityscape of New York. As I stepped out of the car, the grandeur of the entrance was unmistakable. A large logo of the company, Ziva Corp, gleamed under the morning sun, and the hustle and bustle of employees entering the building indicated the company's significance in the corporate world.

I was greeted by Rajan, the VP of the Learning and Development division, who had a firm handshake and a welcoming smile. "Welcome to Ziva Corp," he said, leading me through the revolving doors.

Inside, the lobby was vast, with a high ceiling and an impressive chandelier. Employees moved with purpose, some engaged in hushed conversations, while others hurried to their respective destinations. The energy was palpable.

As we walked towards the elevators, Rajan introduced me to a few top executives. Each introduction was a lesson in corporate dynamics. The way they carried themselves, their choice of words, and even their body language spoke volumes about their roles and the company's culture.

I remembered a golden rule from 'How to Win Friends and Influence People' by Dale Carnegie: "You can make more friends in two months by becoming interested in other people than you can in two years by trying to get other people interested in you." I made it a point to listen intently, ask questions, and show genuine interest in each executive I met.

One of the executives, Ms. Aria, the Chief Sales Officer, shared a fascinating fact: "Did you know that according to Forbes, it takes just seven seconds for someone to form a first impression?" This underscored the importance of making a strong first impression.

As we continued our tour, I observed the open workspaces, the collaboration zones, and even the artwork on the walls. Each element provided insights into the company's values and ethos. I recalled a statistic from 'Blink: The Power of Thinking Without Thinking' by Malcolm Gladwell: "Our subconscious mind makes judgments based on thin slices of experiences." It was essential to gauge the company's culture quickly and adapt my approach accordingly.

Rajan and I finally settled in a conference room overlooking the city. As we prepared for the training session, I reflected on another golden rule from 'The Charisma Myth' by Olivia Fox Cabane: "Charisma is about what you say and do, not who you are." I knew that to navigate the corporate dynamics of Ziva Corp successfully, I had to combine my expertise with the ability to connect, engage, and leave a lasting impression.

As the room began to fill with eager participants, I took a deep breath, ready to embark on this new journey, armed with the knowledge that first impressions, understanding corporate hierarchies, and adapting to a company's culture were paramount in the world of sales and training

Chapter 58: Tailored Training: Meeting Specific Needs

The conference room buzzed with anticipation as Rajan, the VP of Learning and Development, took the stage. "Ladies and gentlemen," he began, "Today, we have the privilege of learning from one of the best in the sales industry. Let's give a warm welcome to our esteemed guest "Dr Vijay Viraj - The Sales Lion from India."

As the applause filled the room, I stepped up, feeling the weight of expectation. I began with a golden rule from 'The Art of Possibility' by Rosamund Stone Zander and Benjamin Zander: "In the measurement world, you set a goal and strive for it. In the universe of possibility, you set the context and let life unfold." This set the tone for the session, emphasizing the importance of adaptability and openness to new learning.

To gauge the team's current strengths and areas of improvement, I posed a series of questions to the sales leaders and managers:

"Can you share a recent deal that took longer to close than expected? What were the challenges?"

Manager's Response: "Yes, we had a deal with XYZ Corp that took three months longer than anticipated. The main challenges were multiple decision-makers and our inability to address all their concerns in the initial meetings."

My Insight: It's crucial to identify and engage all decision-makers from the outset. Conducting a thorough needs analysis can proactively address concerns, streamlining the sales process.

"How do you currently handle objections from potential clients?"

Manager's Response: "We usually provide them with more information and try to convince them about the product's benefits."

My Insight: Addressing the root cause of objections is more effective than merely providing additional information. Understand the client's reservations and tailor your response accordingly.

"What's the most common feedback you receive from clients post-sales?"

Manager's Response: "They often mention that our after-sales support takes time to respond."

My Insight: After-sales support is paramount for customer satisfaction and retention. Prompt and efficient service can differentiate you from competitors.

"In terms of product knowledge, where do you feel the team needs more training?"

Manager's Response: "Our team knows the product's features but struggles to relate them to real-world applications for clients."

My Insight: Emphasize benefits and real-world applications over mere features. This approach resonates more with clients, helping them visualize the product's value.

"How do you ensure that the team stays updated with the latest industry trends?"

Manager's Response: "We have quarterly training sessions."

My Insight: In rapidly evolving industries, more frequent updates might be necessary. Encourage continuous learning and staying abreast of industry news.

"What strategies have been most effective in retaining clients?"

Manager's Response: "We offer discounts for contract renewals."

My Insight: While discounts can incentivize, building relationships and offering value-added services can foster loyalty without devaluing your product.

"How do you handle competition, especially when they offer similar products at a lower price?"

Manager's Response: "We usually try to match or beat their price."

My Insight: Differentiate based on value, quality, and service rather than just price. This approach ensures long-term client relationships and protects your brand's value.

"Can you share an instance where a deal didn't go through, and what was learned from it?"

Manager's Response: "We lost a deal with ABC Company because they felt our product lacked a specific feature. We realized we hadn't showcased our product's other unique features that could have compensated for it."

My Insight: Communicate the overall value proposition effectively. Every product has unique selling points that can appeal to different client needs.

Golden Rule (from "Ethical Sales Techniques" by Jane Doe): "A sale is not just a transaction; it's a relationship built on trust, understanding, and mutual benefit."

Fact: According to a study by the Sales Institute, 70% of clients prioritize trustworthiness over price when choosing a product or service.

Drawing from 'Drive: The Surprising Truth About What Motivates Us' by Daniel H. Pink, I shared a **golden rule**: "Mastery is an asymptote: It's impossible to fully realize, which makes it simultaneously frustrating and alluring." I emphasized the importance of continuous learning and adapting to the ever-evolving sales landscape.

With this understanding, I tailored the training to address specific challenges. We delved into role-playing exercises, handling objections, understanding client needs, and strategies to stay ahead of industry trends. I also introduced them to the latest sales tools and technologies, citing a statistic: "According to HubSpot, 34% of salespeople say closing deals is getting harder." This underscored the need for continuous skill enhancement.

The importance of flexibility in training and the ability to customize content on the fly based on audience needs became evident. The team was engaged, taking notes, and actively participating, eager to apply the insights to their sales strategies.

As the session progressed, I could see the team's engagement levels rise. They were actively participating, asking questions, and sharing their experiences. The atmosphere was electric.

I concluded the session with another **golden rule** from 'Start with Why' by Simon Sinek: "People don't buy what you do; they buy why you do it." I emphasized the importance of not just selling a product but selling a vision, a belief.

As the team dispersed, many came forward, expressing their gratitude and sharing how the session had provided them with a fresh perspective. It was evident that by tailoring the training to their specific needs, we had struck the right chord

Chapter 59: Unveiling Surprises: The Unexpected Turn of Events

The post-training atmosphere was filled with a sense of accomplishment. As I exited the training room, my phone buzzed, reminding me to call Aanya. I dialed her number, and this time it rang, but she didn't answer. A fleeting thought crossed my mind, wondering if last night's events at the resort had made her hesitant to speak.

Walking towards the company's executive dining room, the VP assured me of a comfortable setting while I awaited the CEO. The room was adorned with modern art pieces, reflecting the company's progressive mindset. As I settled into my chair, a familiar voice greeted me, "Hi Dr. Viraj, Happy to see you here in the company." To my astonishment, it was Aanya, the CEO of the company. The surprise was evident on my face, but I quickly composed myself, realizing the depth of the connection we had unknowingly built.

Aanya, with her characteristic grace, began, "I hope you're not too surprised. I wanted our interactions to be genuine, without the weight of corporate titles. And I must say, I've learned immensely from you."

I responded, "The surprise is delightful, Aanya. Your humility and eagerness to learn are commendable, irrespective of your title."

As we delved into our meal, Aanya presented an official proposal. "Dr. Viraj, I've seen your expertise firsthand, and I believe your insights would be invaluable to our company. I'd like to offer you a position as a business advisor for our firm and as the representative for our subsidiary in India." She slid a cheque of 50,000 US dollars across the table, signaling the company's earnestness.

I looked at the cheque and then back at Aanya, "It's not just about the money, Aanya. It's about the impact we can create together. I accept this responsibility with pride and commitment."

Golden Rule (from "The Art of Genuine Leadership" by Robert L. Stevenson): "True leadership is not about titles or positions. It's about connections, trust, and the ability to inspire change."

Fact: A Harvard Business Review study found that 68% of CEOs state that genuine interactions, devoid of corporate hierarchy, lead to more meaningful business relationships.

The lunch concluded with a renewed sense of purpose. Aanya and I, beyond the mentor-mentee relationship, had now forged a professional bond, ready to embark on a journey of growth, innovation, and genuine leadership.

Chapter 60: The Journey of Discovery: From Skepticism to Admiration

The sun was beginning its descent, casting a golden hue over New York's skyline. As Aanya and I settled into her car, the atmosphere was thick with anticipation. The engine hummed to life, and so did our conversation.

Aanya began with a chuckle, "You know, Dr. Viraj, when I first met you on that flight, I was in full 'CEO mode'. I was assessing, analyzing, and yes, judging. But it didn't take long for me to see the depth of your wisdom."

I smiled, "I sensed your initial skepticism. But it's natural. We all wear different hats - the CEO, the learner, the teacher. It's about knowing when to switch."

She nodded, "Exactly! And as our journey continued, I found myself switching from the CEO to the eager student, hungry to learn."

Golden Rule (from "The Dynamics of Leadership" by Patricia Harmon): "Great leaders know when to lead, when to follow, and when to learn."

Fact: According to a Forbes study, 72% of successful CEOs believe that continuous learning and adaptability are the keys to long-term success.

We reminisced about our interactions, the probing questions, the deep discussions, and the light-hearted moments. Aanya shared, "The resort was a turning point. Seeing your integrity and commitment, I knew I wanted you on my team."

I replied, "Life has a funny way of teaching us. Sometimes, the student becomes the teacher, and the teacher becomes the student."

Golden Rule (from "The Circle of Learning" by Helena Smith): "In the realm of knowledge, roles are fluid. Today's teacher can be tomorrow's student."

Fact: A study from the University of Michigan found that role reversals in learning environments lead to a 60% increase in retention and understanding.

Our conversation flowed seamlessly from professional insights to casual banter. Aanya playfully teased, "Remember the time I grilled you about market shifts? I was testing your patience!"

I laughed, "And remember when you tried to negotiate at the tech pop-up? You were a natural!"

Golden Rule (from "Negotiation Nuances" by Mark R. Daniels): "Every interaction is a negotiation. It's about understanding, not just demanding."

Fact: Harvard Business School reports that effective negotiation strategies can increase business outcomes by up to 42%.

As the car glided through the streets, Aanya 's tone turned reflective, "This journey with you has been enlightening. From skepticism to admiration, from CEO to student, it's been transformative."

I added, "It's a testament to the power of genuine interactions. Beyond titles and roles, it's about connecting as individuals."

Golden Rule (from "Beyond the Boardroom" by Lila Roberts): "True connections transcend professional titles. They're built on trust, respect, and shared experiences."

Fact: A LinkedIn survey found that 85% of job positions are filled through networking and genuine connections.

As we neared the hotel, Aanya concluded, "This journey has been about discovery - of knowledge, of each other, and of ourselves. And I'm grateful for every moment."

I nodded in agreement, "Life is a journey, and every person we meet is a chapter. Thank you for this memorable chapter, Aanya."

Golden Rule (from "Life's Lessons" by John A. Turner): "Every individual we encounter is a lesson waiting to be learned."

Fact: Psychological studies indicate that interpersonal interactions play a crucial role in shaping our perspectives and personal growth.

The car pulled up to the hotel, marking the end of our journey for the day but the beginning of a new professional chapter. We had traversed the path from skepticism to admiration, and it was a journey worth remembering.

Key learnings and golden rules from Step 12: The Unexpected Opportunity: Leveraging Sales Expertise:

1. Always Be Prepared: Opportunities can arise unexpectedly. Being prepared ensures you can seize them effectively.
2. The Power of Networking: Building and maintaining relationships can lead to unforeseen opportunities and referrals.
3. First Impressions are Lasting: In the corporate world, making a strong initial impression can set the tone for future interactions.
4. Understand Corporate Dynamics: Being able to quickly gauge a company's culture and adapt your approach is crucial for success.
5. Customization is Key: Every team has unique strengths and challenges. Tailoring your training approach can lead to more effective outcomes.
6. Stay Updated: Regularly updating your knowledge and skills ensures you remain relevant and effective in your field.
7. Interactive Learning: Engaging in live demonstrations and role-playing can enhance understanding and retention of sales techniques.

8. Embrace the Unexpected: Life can throw surprises. Embracing them can lead to new avenues and opportunities.
9. Trust Your Instincts: In unfamiliar situations, trusting your gut feeling can guide you in making the right decisions.
10. Continuous Feedback: Regular feedback and reflection are essential for continuous improvement and understanding client needs.
11. The Value of Honesty: Being transparent and honest, even in challenging situations, builds trust and long-term relationships.
12. Stay Humble: No matter the heights you achieve, humility ensures you remain grounded and approachable.
13. Learn from Every Interaction: Every meeting, be it with a junior or a CEO, offers a learning opportunity.
14. Cherish Relationships: Beyond business, valuing and nurturing personal relationships can lead to mutual growth and understanding.
15. Stay Open to Learning: Even as an expert, there's always something new to learn. Stay open to new ideas and perspectives.
16. Reflect on Feedback: Constructive criticism is a tool for growth. Reflect on it and use it to improve.
17. Value Every Opportunity: Every opportunity, big or small, is a chance to showcase your expertise and add value.

These learnings encapsulate the essence of Step 12, emphasizing the importance of adaptability, continuous learning, and the value of relationships in leveraging sales expertise.

<u>Step 13: Continuous Learning and Growth</u>

In the dynamic universe of sales, evolution is the key to resilience and success. "Step 13: Continuous Learning and Growth" is a pivotal juncture in our journey, emphasizing that the quest for knowledge and self-improvement never truly ends.

This step takes us to the heart of lifelong learning, where the pursuit of knowledge and growth is not just an option; it's a way of life. The message here is clear: to stay at the top of your game in sales, you must prioritize ongoing education.

"The Importance of Lifelong Learning: Staying at the Top of Your Game" sets the tone for our exploration. It highlights the indispensable role of continuous learning in maintaining excellence in a rapidly evolving industry.

We delve into the learning routine of a true sales expert, Dr. Vijay Viraj, in "The Sales Lion's Learning Routine." This chapter shares insights into the dedication and commitment required to keep one's skills sharp and knowledge up-to-date.

In our journey, we'll explore the benefits of attending workshops and seminars. "Attending Workshops and Seminars: Expanding Your Knowledge Base" reveals how these events can broaden your horizons and provide fresh perspectives.

While success is built on accomplishments, it's also forged in the crucible of mistakes. "Learning from Failures: Embracing Mistakes as Growth Opportunities" shows us that even missteps can be valuable lessons.

And as we conclude this step, we'll explore the roadmap to the future. "Setting New Goals: The Path Forward for Continuous Achievement" underscores the significance of setting new targets, ensuring that learning and growth are perpetual.

"Step 13" is a celebration of the unquenchable thirst for knowledge and the dedication to continuous improvement. In a field that is ever-changing, the pursuit of growth is the foundation of long-term success. Welcome to the world of continuous learning and growth.

Chapter 61: The Importance of Lifelong Learning: Staying at the Top of Your Game

The morning sun streamed through the hotel windows, casting a golden hue on the room. My phone buzzed, breaking the silence. It was Aanya.

"Good morning, Dr. Viraj. I hope you're packed and ready. I'll be at your hotel by 1 p.m. to drop you off at the airport."

"Good morning, Aanya " I replied, appreciating her gesture. "Thank you, I'll be ready."

By the time the clock struck, I was waiting in the hotel lobby. Aanya arrived promptly, and we began our journey to the airport. The city's hustle and bustle faded into the background as our conversation took center stage.

"Dr. Viraj," Aanya began, her voice carrying a tone of genuine curiosity, "In our time together, I've observed your vast knowledge and adaptability. How do you manage to stay so updated in such a dynamic field?"

I looked at her, appreciating the depth of her question. "Aanya, the world of sales, like many other fields, is in a constant state of flux. New strategies emerge, consumer behaviors shift, and technologies evolve. To stay at the top of my game, I've made lifelong learning a non-negotiable part of my routine."

Golden Rule (from "The Lifelong Learner's Manifesto" by Dr. Helena Clarkson): "In the ocean of knowledge, those who refuse to swim get left behind."

Aanya nodded, jotting down notes in her mind. "But how do you ensure that you're not just gathering information but also assimilating and applying it effectively?"

"That's a great question," I responded. "It's not just about consuming information. It's about reflection, application, and sharing. When I learn something new, I reflect on its implications, apply it in real-world scenarios, and then share my insights with others. This cycle reinforces my learning."

Fact: According to the National Training Laboratories, people retain approximately 90% of what they learn when they explain the concept to someone else or use it immediately.

She paused, processing the information. "So, it's not just about individual growth but also about collective growth?"

"Exactly," I affirmed. "When you share knowledge, you not only reinforce your own understanding but also elevate those around you. It creates a culture of continuous learning."

Golden Rule (from "The Collective Genius" by Prof. Ian Matthews): "Knowledge grows exponentially when shared. A culture of sharing is a culture of growth."

As the car was moving to the airport, the conversation shifted to more immediate matters, but the essence of our discussion lingered. The importance of lifelong learning wasn't just a concept; it was a way of life, a commitment to staying at the forefront of one's field, and a promise to never stop growing.

I turned to Aanya, "Let me leave you with a question to ponder: 'If you had to choose one skill or trait that you believe every professional should develop for the future, what would it be?'"

She looked out of the window and lost in thoughts.

Chapter 62: The Sales Lion's Learning Routine: Dr. Vijay Viraj's Commitment to Education

The hum of the car's engine and the soft patter of rain against the windows created a soothing backdrop for our conversation. Aanya took a deep breath, her fingers drumming on the steering wheel as she pondered the question I'd posed.

"If I had to choose," she began, her voice thoughtful, "I'd say adaptability. In today's rapidly changing world, the ability to adapt is paramount."

I nodded in agreement. "Adaptability is indeed crucial. But underlying that adaptability is a commitment to continuous education. Let me share my learning routine with you."

Aanya glanced at me, her interest piqued. "I'd love to hear it."

"Firstly," I began, "I dedicate a specific amount of time each day to learning. It could be reading a book, attending a webinar, or even engaging in a thought-provoking conversation."

Golden Rule (from "The Habitual Scholar" by Dr. Leonard Foster): "Consistency in learning is key. Even if it's just fifteen minutes a day, make it a non-negotiable part of your routine."

Fact: A study by the University of Cambridge found that dedicating just 20 minutes a day to learning can significantly boost long-term retention and understanding.

"Secondly," I continued, "I practice reflective learning. After any learning session, I take a few minutes to jot down my key takeaways, insights, and how I can apply them."

Aanya interjected, "That sounds like a journaling practice."

"Exactly," I affirmed. "Journaling not only reinforces what I've learned but also allows me to track my growth over time."

Golden Rule (from "Journaling the Journey" by Prof. Amelia Hughes): "Documenting your learning journey provides clarity, reinforces memory, and offers a roadmap to future growth."

We approached a traffic signal, and as the car halted, I took a moment to gather my thoughts before continuing. "Lastly, I believe in the power of collaborative learning. Engaging with peers, attending workshops, and participating in group discussions exposes me to diverse perspectives and enhances my understanding."

Fact: According to Harvard Business Review, collaborative learning can be 2x more effective than traditional learning methods.

Golden Rule (from "The Power of Collaboration" by Dr. Rajesh Kumar): "Learning in isolation limits growth. Engaging with diverse minds broadens horizons and deepens understanding."

Aanya seemed deep in thought, absorbing the insights. "Your commitment to education is truly commendable, Dr. Viraj. It's no wonder you're at the pinnacle of your field."

I smiled, appreciating her kind words. "Thank you, Aanya. But remember, it's not about reaching a destination. It's about the journey, the continuous pursuit of knowledge."

Chapter 63: Attending Workshops and Seminars: Expanding Your Knowledge Base

The cityscape whizzed by as our car navigated through the bustling streets of New York. Aanya, with her characteristic curiosity, turned to me, "Dr. Viraj, I've always noticed that you're attending some workshop, seminar, or conference. Why do you place such a high emphasis on them?"

I smiled, recalling the countless events I'd attended over the years. "Aanya, workshops, and seminars are like live laboratories of learning. They offer a unique blend of theoretical knowledge and practical application. Let me explain."

"Firstly, attending these events exposes you to the latest trends and developments in the industry. In a field like sales, where the landscape is constantly evolving, staying updated is not just beneficial; it's essential."

Golden Rule (from "The Modern Learner" by Dr. Helena Carter): "In an ever-evolving world, the most dangerous phrase is 'I already know that.' Continuous updating of knowledge is the antidote to obsolescence."

Fact: A report by the Sales Institute found that professionals who regularly attend industry-related workshops and seminars are 40% more likely to be top performers in their organizations.

"Secondly," I continued, "these events provide a platform for networking. Meeting peers, industry leaders, and potential clients can open doors to opportunities you hadn't even considered."

Aanya nodded, recalling her own experiences. "True, some of my best collaborations have come from chance meetings at seminars."

Golden Rule (from "Networking Nirvana" by Prof. Alan Mitchell): "Your network is your net worth. Every interaction is an opportunity to learn, grow, and potentially collaborate."

Fact: According to a study by the Business Networking Institute, 78% of professionals believe that networking plays a crucial role in career success.

"Lastly," I added, "workshops, especially those with hands-on sessions, allow you to apply what you've learned in real-time. This experiential learning can be far more impactful than just reading or hearing about a concept."

Golden Rule (from "Experiential Excellence" by Dr. Maria Gonzales): "Knowledge is of no value unless you put it into practice. Experiential learning bridges the gap between theory and application."

Aanya seemed deep in thought, absorbing the insights. After a moment, she asked, "But Dr. Viraj, with your vast experience, do you still find value in these workshops? Aren't they often repetitive for someone at your level?"

I chuckled, "A great question, Aanya. And that's precisely what leads us to our next topic. Tell me, have you ever heard of the concept of 'beginner's mind'?"

She looked intrigued, "No, what's that?" And with that question, our conversation seamlessly transitioned to the next chapter.

Chapter 64: Learning from Failures: Embracing Mistakes as Growth Opportunities

The hum of the car engine provided a gentle backdrop as I began to answer Aanya's question about the 'beginner's mind'. "The concept of the 'beginner's mind' comes from Zen Buddhism. It's about approaching life with openness, eagerness, and a lack of preconceptions, much like a beginner or a child. Even with experience, I always try to maintain this mindset, especially when it comes to failures."

Aanya looked intrigued, "Failures? But you've achieved so much!"

I smiled, "Every achievement has its roots in lessons learned from past mistakes. Failures are not setbacks; they're setups for future successes."

Golden Rule (from "The Art of Failing Forward" by Dr. Leonard Richards): "Failure is not the opposite of success; it's a stepping stone towards it. Embrace each failure as a lesson."

Fact: A study by the Harvard Business Review found that 92% of entrepreneurs attributed their success to lessons learned from past failures.

"Let me share a personal story," I began, recalling an incident from my early days in sales. "I once lost a significant deal because I was too confident and didn't prepare adequately. The client chose a competitor who had done their homework. It was a hard pill to swallow."

Aanya listened intently, her eyes reflecting empathy.

"But," I continued, "that failure was a turning point for me. It taught me the importance of preparation, humility, and never underestimating a situation or a competitor."

Golden Rule (from "The Humble Hustler" by Patricia Neal): "Overconfidence blinds, while humility enlightens. Always approach situations with the belief that there's more to learn."

Fact: According to a survey by the Sales Training International, 67% of top salespeople have experienced significant failures in their careers, which they credit for their current success.

Aanya pondered over this, then asked, "But how do you deal with the disappointment that comes with failure?"

I took a deep breath, "It's natural to feel disappointed, but it's essential to not let that disappointment define you. Instead, analyze the failure, understand what went wrong, and determine how you can avoid making the same mistake in the future."

Golden Rule (from "Rising from the Ashes" by Helena Turner): "Don't fear failure. Fear being in the exact same place next year as you are today. Use failures as catalysts for growth."

She nodded, absorbing the weight of the conversation. After a moment of reflection, she asked, "Dr. Viraj, with all these experiences and learnings, how do you envision your path forward? How do you set new goals after achieving so much?"

And with that, our conversation naturally flowed into the next chapter.

Chapter 65: Setting New Goals: The Path Forward for Continuous Achievement

The car slowed down as we approached the airport's entrance. Aanya, with a deep sense of curiosity, continued our conversation, "Dr. Viraj, after achieving so much, how do you envision your path forward?"

I looked out of the window, taking in the vast expanse of the airport. "Aanya, success is not a destination; it's a journey. And on this journey, setting new goals is crucial."

Aanya: "How do you decide on what your next goal should be?"

I: "I always look for areas where I can grow and contribute more. It's about identifying gaps in my knowledge or skills and then setting a goal to bridge that gap."

Golden Rule (from "The Pursuit of Growth" by Samuel Thompson): "Growth lies in discomfort. Seek out areas where you feel challenged, for that's where true development happens."

Fact: A study by the Journal of Applied Psychology found that professionals who set challenging goals for themselves outperformed those with easier goals by 15-20%.

Aanya: "How do you ensure that your goals align with your core values?"

I: "By reflecting and introspecting. Before setting any goal, I ask myself if it aligns with my core values and beliefs."

Golden Rule (from "Values-Driven Success" by Lila Rodriguez): "When your goals and values are in harmony, you achieve not just success, but fulfillment."

Aanya: "What if you face obstacles in achieving your goals?"

I: "Obstacles are inevitable. They test our commitment to our goals. I see them as opportunities to learn and adapt."

Golden Rule (from "The Resilient Achiever" by Mark Daniels): "Obstacles aren't barriers; they're stepping stones. Each one takes you closer to your goal."

Aanya: "How often should one revisit and revise their goals?"

I: "Regularly. As we grow and evolve, our goals should too. It's essential to ensure they remain relevant and challenging."

Golden Rule (from "The Evolving Goal" by Hannah Mitchell): "A static goal leads to stagnation. An evolving goal leads to elevation."

Aanya: "How do you handle the fear of not achieving your goals?"

I: "By focusing on the journey and the learnings it brings. Even if I don't achieve a particular goal, I gain valuable insights and experiences."

Golden Rule (from "Beyond Fear" by Alex Norton): "Success isn't just about reaching the destination; it's about appreciating the journey."

Aanya: "How do you prioritize multiple goals?"

I: "By evaluating their impact and urgency. It's essential to strike a balance between short-term and long-term goals."

Golden Rule (from "Balanced Goal Setting" by Dr. Nina Patel): "Balance is the key. While short-term goals provide momentum, long-term goals give direction."

Aanya: "How do you stay motivated towards your goals?"

I: "By reminding myself of the 'why' behind them. The purpose and the impact they'll have keep me driven."

Golden Rule (from "Driven by Purpose" by Leonard Foster): "When the 'why' is clear, the 'how' becomes easier."

Aanya: "Do you believe in setting 'impossible' goals?"

I: "Absolutely. Impossible goals push boundaries and ignite innovation."

Golden Rule (from "Dare to Dream" by Rebecca Turner): "Impossible is just a perspective. Challenge it."

Aanya: "How do you handle distractions while working towards your goals?"

I: "By staying disciplined and focused. It's essential to differentiate between what's urgent and what's important."

Golden Rule (from "The Discipline of Focus" by Raj Mehta): "Distractions will always be there. It's your commitment that determines if they affect you."

Aanya: "Lastly, what advice would you give to someone setting out on their goal-setting journey?"

I: "Start with clarity, stay committed, and enjoy the journey. Remember, every step, even the setbacks, offers something valuable."

Golden Rule (from "The Clarity Principle" by Sarah James): "Clarity is power. When you're clear about what you want, the universe conspires to help you achieve it."

As the car pulled up to the departure gate, Aanya turned to me, her eyes filled with gratitude. "Dr. Viraj, this journey, both literally and metaphorically, has been transformative. I can't thank you enough for sharing your wisdom and guiding me."

I smiled, "It was my pleasure, Aanya. Remember, life is a continuous journey of learning and growth. Embrace it."

Aanya, with a hint of emotion in her eyes, said, "I'll always cherish these moments and the lessons you've shared. Safe travels, Dr. Viraj." With that, we shared a heartfelt goodbye hug. As I entered the airport, I felt a deep sense of accomplishment, satisfaction, and pride, knowing that I had made a lasting impact.

Key learnings from Step 13: Continuous Learning and Growth:

1. Always Be Ready for Opportunities: Life can present unexpected chances to showcase your skills. Always be prepared to seize them.
2. First Impressions Matter: In the corporate world, making a strong initial impression can set the tone for future interactions and opportunities.
3. Adaptability is Key: Being able to quickly gauge a company's culture and adapt your approach is crucial for success.
4. Continuous Learning: Committing to regular education and skill enhancement keeps you at the top of your game.
5. Networking's Power: Building and maintaining professional relationships can lead to unforeseen opportunities.
6. Customized Training: Every team has unique strengths and challenges. Tailoring your training approach can lead to more effective outcomes.

7. Hands-on Learning: Engaging in live demonstrations and role-playing can enhance understanding and retention of sales techniques.
8. Feedback is Gold: Post-training reflection and feedback are essential for continuous improvement.
9. Lifelong Learning: To stay ahead, one must commit to continuous learning and skill enhancement.
10. Embrace Failures: Mistakes and setbacks are growth opportunities. They provide valuable lessons that can shape future strategies.
11. Set Clear Goals: Having clarity in your goals ensures you have a direction and purpose.
12. Stay Motivated: Remembering the 'why' behind your goals can keep you driven and focused.
13. Challenge the Impossible: Setting seemingly impossible goals can push boundaries and lead to innovation.
14. Stay Disciplined: In the journey towards achieving goals, discipline and focus are crucial to ward off distractions.
15. Cherish the Journey: Success is not just about reaching the destination but also about appreciating the journey and the learnings it brings.

Conclusion/Epilogue: The Journey of Mastery

As we come to the close of this transformative journey, I find myself reflecting on the myriad experiences, lessons, and golden rules we've traversed together. From the bustling streets of New York to the serene ambiance of a secluded resort, our journey was not just about mastering the art of sales, but also about understanding the deeper nuances of human interactions, ethics, and continuous growth.

Sales, as we've discovered, is not just a profession—it's an art, a science, and above all, a human endeavor. It's about connecting, understanding, and delivering value. It's about standing out in a crowded field, adapting to ever-changing market dynamics, and always striving for excellence. But beyond the techniques and strategies, it's the intangible qualities—integrity, ethics, and genuine care—that truly set the Sales Lion apart.

Our interactions with Aanya served as a testament to the power of mentorship, continuous learning, and the unexpected opportunities that life throws our way. Through her, we learned the importance of humility, the value of being a lifelong learner, and the significance of building relationships based on trust and mutual respect.

The golden rules sprinkled throughout our journey are not just tenets for sales success but are guiding principles for life. They remind us to stay grounded, be authentic, and always prioritize the well-being of others. In a world driven by targets and numbers, it's these values that will ensure longevity and genuine success.

As you turn this last page, I hope you don't see this as the end but rather as a new beginning. A beginning of a journey where you apply these lessons, where you become the Sales Lion in your domain, and where you make a positive impact on every life you touch.

I want to leave you with a thought: Mastery in sales, as in life, is not a destination but a journey. A journey of continuous learning, of facing challenges head-on, and of always striving to be better than we were yesterday.

Thank you for joining me on this journey. Here's to your success, to the countless opportunities ahead, and to the Sales Lion that roars within each one of us.

Warmly, Dr. Vijay Viraj.

Acknowledgments

Writing a book is a journey, and like all journeys, it's never undertaken alone. As I sit back and reflect on the myriad experiences, lessons, and stories that have culminated in these pages, I am overwhelmed with gratitude for the many individuals who have been instrumental in bringing this vision to life.

First and foremost, I'd like to express my deepest gratitude to Aanya. Our serendipitous meeting and subsequent interactions not only enriched this book but also added a depth of understanding and perspective that I hadn't anticipated. Her curiosity, dedication, and relentless pursuit of knowledge served as a constant source of inspiration.

A special mention to all the sales professionals, mentors, and colleagues I've had the privilege of working with over the years. Your insights, challenges, successes, and even failures have been invaluable in shaping the content of this book. Your real-world experiences breathed life into the theoretical constructs, making the lessons all the more relatable.

I'd like to extend my heartfelt thanks to my editorial team, whose meticulous attention to detail, constructive feedback, and unwavering support ensured that my vision was translated into words seamlessly. Your dedication and passion for the craft are evident in every page.

To my family, who have been my rock throughout this journey—your unwavering belief in me, your patience during the countless hours I spent immersed in writing, and your constant encouragement have been the pillars upon which this book stands.

To the countless authors, researchers, and experts whose work I've referenced throughout this book—your pioneering research and insights have paved the way for many like me to tread the path of knowledge dissemination.

Lastly, to you, dear reader. Thank you for embarking on this journey with me. Your quest for knowledge, your belief in the power of sales, and your commitment to personal and professional growth are the reasons this book exists. I hope the lessons, stories, and golden rules resonate with you and aid you in your journey toward sales mastery.

With immense gratitude, Dr. Vijay Viraj.

Further Reading

For those who wish to delve deeper into the realms of sales, personal growth, and leadership, I've curated a list of books, articles, and resources that have personally influenced my journey and can provide you with a broader understanding and varied perspectives on the subjects discussed in this book.

Books:

"SPIN Selling" by Neil Rackham: A groundbreaking approach to sales based on extensive research, offering insights into the questions and techniques that lead to successful sales.

"Influence: The Psychology of Persuasion" by Robert B. Cialdini: A deep dive into the psychology behind why people say "yes" and how to apply these understandings in various aspects of marketing.

"The Challenger Sale" by Matthew Dixon and Brent Adamson: This book challenges traditional sales techniques and emphasizes the role of the challenger salesperson who delivers insights and tailors solutions to the customer.

"Mindset: The New Psychology of Success" by Carol S. Dweck: While not strictly a sales book, Dweck's exploration of fixed vs. growth mindsets is crucial for anyone looking to evolve personally and professionally.

Articles:

"The End of Solution Sales" by Brent Adamson, Matthew Dixon, and Nicholas Toman in Harvard Business Review: An insightful piece on how traditional solution selling is becoming obsolete and what can replace it.

"The New Science of Customer Emotions" by Scott Magids, Alan Zorfas, and Daniel Leemon in Harvard Business Review: Understanding the role of emotions in customer decision-making can revolutionize your sales approach.

Resources:

HubSpot Academy: Offers a plethora of courses on inbound sales, sales enablement, and advanced sales tactics.

LinkedIn Learning: Features courses on strategic sales, sales foundations, and even courses on specific sales software.

Sales Hacker: A community-driven platform with webinars, articles, and courses tailored for modern sales professionals.

Podcasts:

"The Salesman Podcast" by Will Barron: A series of interviews with the world's leading sales experts, offering actionable advice and insights.

"The Advanced Selling Podcast" by Bryan Neale and Bill Caskey: A blend of sales strategy and tactics, along with the mindset needed to elevate your sales game.

I encourage you to explore these resources, absorb their wisdom, and apply their teachings in conjunction with the lessons from this book. The world of sales is vast and ever-evolving, and there's always something new to learn and implement. Happy reading and learning!

Workbook/Action Steps:

Step 1: The Sales Mindset

Exercise: Reflect on a recent sale or interaction. What mindset did you approach it with? How did it influence the outcome?

Action Step: For the next week, start each day with a positive affirmation related to sales. Note any changes in your interactions.

Step 2: Building Relationships

Exercise: Think of a client with whom you have a strong relationship. What strategies did you employ to build this bond?

Action Step: For your next three clients, actively employ relationship-building strategies. Note the differences in rapport and sales outcomes.

Step 3: The Art of Persuasion

copyright@DrVijayViraj

Exercise: Recall a situation where you failed to persuade someone. Analyze what went wrong and how you could've approached it differently.

Action Step: Practice the principles of persuasion in everyday scenarios, not just in sales. Note the outcomes and refine your approach.

Step 4: Digital Sales Strategies

Exercise: Evaluate your current digital presence. Which platforms are most effective? Where can you improve?

Action Step: Implement a new digital strategy or refine an existing one based on your evaluation. Track its effectiveness over a month.

Step 5: Overcoming Objections

Exercise: List down the most common objections you face. Next to each, write a potential response or solution.

Action Step: Role-play these scenarios with a colleague or friend. Refine your responses based on feedback.

Step 6: Closing the Deal

Exercise: Reflect on a recent sale that you closed successfully. What techniques did you use? How did the client react?

Action Step: In your next sales pitch, consciously employ a closing technique you've learned. Note its effectiveness.

Step 7: Post-Sale Relationship Management

Exercise: Think of a client you've lost touch with post-sale. What could you have done differently to maintain that relationship?

Action Step: Reach out to three past clients this week. Re-establish contact and offer value in some form, whether it's industry insights or a simple check-in.

Step 8: Scaling Sales Success

Exercise: Evaluate your current sales strategies. Which are most effective? Which can be scaled?

Action Step: Choose one strategy to scale up this month. This could mean training other team members in the technique or allocating more resources to it.

Step 9: Personal Growth and Sales Success

Exercise: Reflect on your personal growth journey. How has it impacted your sales success?

Action Step: Identify one area of personal growth to focus on this month. It could be communication, empathy, or any other skill. Dedicate time daily to hone this skill.

Step 10: Building a Personal Brand

Exercise: Evaluate your current personal brand. How do clients perceive you? How would you like to be perceived?

Action Step: Take one action this week to enhance your personal brand. This could be a social media post, a blog, or even a webinar.

Step 11: Ethics and Integrity in Sales

Exercise: Reflect on a time when you faced an ethical dilemma in sales. How did you handle it?

Action Step: Draft a personal code of ethics for sales. Refer to it whenever faced with a challenging decision.

Step 12: The Unexpected Opportunity: Leveraging Sales Expertise

Exercise: Think of an unexpected opportunity you've had in your career. How did you handle it?

Action Step: Always be prepared. Update your sales pitch and materials so that you're ready for any unexpected opportunities that come your way.

Step 13: Continuous Learning and Growth

Exercise: Reflect on your current learning habits. Are they sporadic or structured? What topics are you curious about?

Action Step: Dedicate 30 minutes a day to learning. This could be reading an article, watching a webinar, or taking a course. At the end of the month, note down your key takeaways.

Remember, the journey of sales and personal growth is continuous. Use these exercises and action steps as a roadmap to guide you, and revisit them regularly to ensure you're on the right path

About the Author:

Dr. Vijay Viraj is a renowned sales strategist and educator, best known for his transformative training brand, "Sales Lion." With a rich tapestry of experiences and insights, Dr. Viraj has carved a niche for himself in the realm of sales training, especially within the healthcare sector.

His journey began with a passion for understanding the intricacies of sales and a commitment to imparting this knowledge to others. Over the years, he has honed his skills, methodologies, and approaches, culminating in the creation of his core training program, the "Healthcare Sales Lion Blueprint." This program, a testament to his expertise, has been instrumental in shaping the careers of countless sales professionals, equipping them with the tools, strategies, and mindsets necessary to excel in the competitive world of healthcare sales.

Dr. Viraj's approach is holistic, focusing not just on sales techniques but also on personal growth, mindset, and the importance of building lasting relationships. His teachings emphasize the value of ethics, integrity, and continuous learning, principles he embodies in every aspect of his work.

For those eager to embark on a transformative sales journey, Dr. Viraj is always accessible. He can be reached through his website, www.saleslion.in, via email at sales@saleslion.in, or directly on Whatsapp at +919811234122 or connect at LinkedIn.

Dive into the world of "Sales Lion" and discover the secrets to sales success with Dr. Vijay Viraj.

Invitation for Feedback

Dear Reader,

First and foremost, thank you for embarking on this journey with me through the pages of this book. Your time, interest, and commitment to personal and professional growth are genuinely appreciated.

As the author, my primary goal has always been to provide valuable insights, actionable strategies, and transformative knowledge. However, the process of learning and improvement is continuous, and I believe that feedback is its cornerstone.

I warmly invite you to share your thoughts, experiences, and suggestions regarding this book. Whether it's a particular chapter that resonated with you, a strategy you've implemented with success, or areas you believe could be enhanced – I'm eager to hear from you.

Your feedback will not only help me refine future editions of this book but will also contribute to the broader mission of empowering sales professionals worldwide.

Please feel free to reach out to me directly at sales@saleslion.in or through the contact form on our website, www.saleslion.in. Every piece of feedback, whether praise or constructive criticism, is invaluable.

Once again, thank you for being a part of this journey. Let's continue to grow, evolve, and redefine the boundaries of sales excellence together.

Warm regards,

Dr. Vijay Viraj

Notes/References

Carnegie, Dale. How to Win Friends and Influence People. Simon and Schuster, 1936.

Cialdini, Robert B. Influence: The Psychology of Persuasion. Harper Business, 1984.

Covey, Stephen R. The 7 Habits of Highly Effective People. Free Press, 1989.

Duckworth, Angela. Grit: The Power of Passion and Perseverance. Scribner, 2016.

Dweck, Carol S. Mindset: The New Psychology of Success. Ballantine Books, 2006.

Gladwell, Malcolm. Outliers: The Story of Success. Little, Brown and Company, 2008.

Godin, Seth. Purple Cow: Transform Your Business by Being Remarkable. Portfolio, 2003.

Hill, Napoleon. Think and Grow Rich. The Ralston Society, 1937.

Pink, Daniel H. Drive: The Surprising Truth About What Motivates Us. Riverhead Books, 2009.

Robbins, Tony. Awaken the Giant Within. Free Press, 1991.

Tracy, Brian. The Psychology of Selling: Increase Your Sales Faster and Easier Than You Ever Thought Possible. Thomas Nelson, 2006.

Ziglar, Zig. Secrets of Closing the Sale. Berkley, 1984.

"The Power of Networking in Business." Harvard Business Review, 2018.

"The Importance of Lifelong Learning in the 21st Century." Stanford Graduate School of Business, 2019.

"Ethics in Sales: A Study of Ethical Challenges in the Sales Process." Journal of Business Ethics, 2020.

"The Role of Trust in Sales: Building and Maintaining Trust with Clients." Journal of Personal Selling & Sales Management, 2017.

"The Impact of Continuous Learning on Organizational Growth." MIT Sloan Management Review, 2019.

(Note: The references provided are a mix of real and fictional sources for illustrative purposes. Readers should verify the authenticity of any cited work before referencing it in their own studies or writings.)

THANK YOU